Books by

LOGAN PEARSALL SMITH

✶

UNFORGOTTEN YEARS

Unforgotten Years

LOGAN
PEARSALL
SMITH

Published *in* BOSTON *by*

LITTLE, BROWN AND COMPANY

1939

THE ATLANTIC MONTHLY PRESS BOOKS
ARE PUBLISHED BY
LITTLE, BROWN AND COMPANY
IN ASSOCIATION WITH
THE ATLANTIC MONTHLY COMPANY

PRINTED IN THE UNITED STATES OF AMERICA

CONTENTS

UNFORGOTTEN YEARS

1

Boyhood and Youth

WE ARE ANCHORED at Phalerum; how can I spend the morning better than in beginning to write my reminiscences? My hostess is, I believe, writing hers in her stateroom above; I think I shall follow her example. Hers will sell by the thousands, for she is a famous writer; I cannot hope for an interest like this in mine, but there may be people who will like to look at them, and I shall enjoy calling back the past. Certainly I shan't read them to my friendly but extremely critical companions on this cruise. For one thing there won't be time; our days are spent in looking at the Ægean Islands, or in seeing sights on shore. In the evening we sit on deck and talk; or, if the wind is blowing, we listen in the cabin to Robert Norton's reading of Butcher and

Lang's translation of the *Odyssey*, and beautifully he reads it.

So with this brief preface I begin the record of my boyhood and youth, to which I may add, if the spirit moves me, a few of the experiences of my later years.

It is the custom of good Americans to bestow, somewhat in the Chinese fashion, a kind of posthumous nobility upon their ancestors; to transform the farmers and small tradesmen from whom they are almost all descended into scions of great, historic English houses. This innocent exercise of the fancy produces a good deal of blameless satisfaction, since there is indeed, I believe, a more abiding sense of noble birth to be derived from false than from authentic pedigrees; and plebeian blood flows with a more consciously aristocratic thrill through the veins of those who have dyed it in the azure of their own imaginations.

It is not for me, at least, to reprobate such delusions, for was I not nourished in my

[4]

youth upon them? Had not certain elderly and imaginative members of my family succeeded, after long meditation, in adorning the mediocrity of their circumstances with at least one escutcheon, in tracing one portion of their line to aristocratic sources?

Of the plebeian lineage and name of Smith they could indeed make little; the Smiths were only too plainly a race of Yorkshire yeoman farmers, who, becoming Quakers, had emigrated to New Jersey in the time of William Penn, and, settling in the quiet town of Burlington on the Delaware, had engaged in commerce with the West Indies, watching the broad river for the arrival of small brigantines or "snows," which sailed thither, laden with the products of the South. But one of them in the eighteenth century, my grandfather's grandfather, with the respectable name of John Smith, had married a daughter of the secretary whom William Penn had brought to Pennsylvania and left there as his representative.

This secretary, James Logan, was, so history says, the son of a schoolmaster of Scottish descent at Lurgan in the north of Ireland. When the troubles of the civil war drove the family to Bristol, young Logan was apprenticed to a linen draper, but became afterwards a master in the school his father started there. This father belonged to a respectable Scottish family and neither he nor his son claimed a nobler derivation. In the creative imagination of their descendants in America, however, they became members of a noble and famous race, the Logans of Restalrig, and owners of that Fast Castle which was described by Scott in *The Bride of Lammermoor* as the house of Ravenswood. One of the Logans had gone to Palestine as a Crusader, to convey thither the heart of Robert Bruce, and another had been hanged, centuries later, for his participation in the Gowrie Conspiracy.

This background of crusades and crimes, with imaginary castles and gallows in the distance, shed a kind of glamour on the lives of these mild Quakers, who, in spite of the

Quaker ban on worldly fiction, must, it appears, have been reading *Waverley Novels* on the sly. And was it not for them all perfectly authentic? Had not one of them crossed the Atlantic and made a special pilgrimage to Scotland, and there, on the spot, when visiting the estate of this famous family, been overcome by a profound conviction of its truth? Was not the heart of Bruce which adorned the arms of the Restalrig family (arms which James Logan had never dreamt of assuming) — was not this bleeding heart splashed upon the note paper and engraved upon the silver of the family in Philadelphia? What genealogist could demand, what documents could provide, more convincing evidence than this?

These imagined glories rather obscured in the eyes of his descendants their ancestor's real distinction; for William Penn's secretary had become the most remarkable inhabitant of the English colonies during the first half of the eighteenth century. Remaining in Pennsylvania as the agent for William Penn and his sons, he held in turn every important office in that commonwealth. He was the master of many languages, and an authority also on mathematics and astronomy, and as a botanist he made an important contribution to the theory of the sexuality of plants. He corresponded with learned men all over Europe, and collected the finest library in America, containing all the best books on history, on art and geography, of the time, as well as all the Latin and Greek classics, including Bentley's editions. He transformed Philadelphia in fact into the Athens of America, as it was called; and it was thither that Benjamin Franklin fled in his youth from a less cultivated Boston. Of Franklin and his printing press he was one of the earliest patrons, and Franklin printed for him two of his translations from Cicero, in one of which, described as the first translation made in America from the classics, the young printer expressed a hope that "this first translation of a classic in the Western world might be a happy omen that Philadelphia shall become the seat of the Muses." This hope, I may note in passing, has not been yet fulfilled, though my ancestor did his best to prepare for the advent of the Nine to the Quaker city, by bequeathing his books to the Philadelphia Library which Benjamin Franklin founded there.

In the meantime his son-in-law, the John Smith I have mentioned, occupied himself in a prosperous commerce with the West Indies, exchanging grain, lumber, and other products of the North for sugar, rum, and molasses from the South. These were transported in his own vessels, built in his own shipyard at Burlington, and sailing from the wharf there which he owned. After publishing in Philadelphia, where he dwelt, a pamphlet in defense of the pacifist principles of the Quakers, he had retired to the family home at Burlington, up the river, and spent the rest of his life in reading and, as his grandson, my grandfather, put it, in "copying into commonplace books those sentiments and sententious remarks of favorite authors which he approved." This taste for copying out was shared by his family and descendants. His brother, Samuel Smith, compiled from many documents a history of New Jersey which is still, I believe, cited by those who are interested in that subject; his son, who inherited the name of John Smith, inherited this taste also and filled several volumes with the lives and memorable sayings of New Jersey Quakers; his grandson, who was my grandfather, published many colonial documents; and I too, with the various documents and anthologies I have published, have not failed in carrying on this family tradition.

I like to think of that lot of quiet and bookish old forbears, among whom was at least one minor poet, settled on the banks of the Delaware among the wigwams and papooses of the Indians, thinking their mild Quaker thoughts in their meetinghouses, or listening to the preaching of John Woolman, who also lived at Burlington, and was their friend and neighbor. They seem to have been content to spend their lives in this Quaker Arcadia, fishing in the broad river which flowed past their farms, or reading the books which trickled over to them across the Atlantic, and copying out sententious extracts from those eighteenth-century volumes.

My grandfather, however, John Jay Smith, left Burlington as a boy, and sailing down the Delaware to Philadelphia, establishing himself there first as a chemist's assistant, soon began to engage in other activities. Among the stipulations which James Logan had made in bequeathing his books to the Philadelphia Library was one to the effect that his eldest son should be the librarian, and his eldest grandson in the male line should succeed; and should the male line fail, the position should be offered to the eldest of the female line. To my grandfather this appointment was given; he occupied it many years, and was succeeded in it by one of my uncles. James Logan's will was, I believe, invalid; the position thus dubiously bequeathed was a modest one; but since it was held for more than fifty years by members of our family,

our claim to this humble librarianship came
to be regarded, at least by ourselves, as con-
ferring a kind of dim distinction; and it was
originally intended that I should succeed my
uncle (who had no son) in this, as we imagi-
natively designated it, the only hereditary
office in America.

It was from this old Philadelphia Library,
an eighteenth-century building in the neighborhood of Independence Square, with its air
of venerable antiquity, — for the few old
buildings found in a new country seem to possess a more antique aspect than anything in
Europe, — it was in this old library, long
since destroyed, with its dim interior and old
folios and bewigged portraits, that I received
my first bookish impressions, being often
taken there as a little boy, and given a book to
read by my uncle who presided over the silence of that unfrequented institution. Thus
in my earliest years I became familiar with
the atmosphere of old libraries, and the dim
light that dwells in them, and fell under the
spell which they cast upon those who haunt

their precincts — that quietness, that hush of the human spirit in the ghostly presence of its own immortality, stored up in rows of ancient volumes and great folios of the classics.

But I anticipate, perhaps, my more romantic impressions of this kind. It was in this library at least that, encouraged by my librarian uncle, I first formed the habit of reading. What that habit might grow into was impressed upon me by my occasional visits to the aged ex-librarian, my grandfather, at the house to which he had retired in the Quaker suburb of Germantown, where he lived to a great old age, spending his days in his study upstairs, with his gouty toe on a cushion, reading and reading all day long. "I believe it may be safely said," he wrote of himself towards the end of his life, "that for forty years, eight hours of every day, or nearly so, have been employed in reading of the most miscellaneous character, often the best books, but too often the lighter kind." When I happened, not long ago, upon this sentence in my grandfather's *Recollections*, I was struck by the accurate description it gave of my own existence, which for the last forty years or so has been spent, like his, in miscellaneous reading, and often too, like his, "of the lighter kind." The analogy was a curious one; indeed, I found it more curious than pleasing; for recalling my visits to that old gentleman, I turned my eyes on my elderly self, where I sat reading upstairs, and saw myself for a disconcerting moment. And then I went on reading.

It might have increased my awe of my grandfather had I known, as I now know, that he had every right to the designation of a retired pirate, since a large portion of his earlier years had been spent in the occupation of pirating the works of famous English writers. Indeed, he has some claim to be the earliest of these pirates, since, as the *Dictionary of American Biography* states, he suggested in 1832 to Adam Waldie, a Philadelphia printer, the republication, in the absence of international copyright, of important foreign books, and became the editor of *Waldie's*

Select Circulating Library, in which many English books were reprinted for American readers, without any thought of remunerating their authors. This became finally an international crime and scandal; and if I cannot boast of descent from any Scottish criminals, I may at least claim that my grandfather was the first of American literary pirates. But he incurred no blame among his contemporaries, and writes freely of these activities in his printed *Recollections*. The thing, however, which was the subject of reprobation in his lifetime, and which, reaching my ears in dark references and whispers, much increased the terror of my visits to him, was the dreadful fact that he was an "Unbeliever." What exactly an Unbeliever was, and what he disbelieved in, I had not the dimmest notion, but I knew that his future was thereby involved in the most dreadful consequences; and I remember a sense of the removal of an impending calamity when it was generally agreed that, by a deathbed conversion, this dark cloud had been lifted from the old gentleman's prospects in the future world.

More definite and more terrifying is the memory of one dreadful occasion when, not long before his death, my grandfather, who seldom left his study, hobbled downstairs and, establishing himself in his drawing-room, began to denounce the age, uttering sentiments of a kind that sounded incredible in my ears. The theme of his discourse — it is a theme which is familiar, perhaps too familiar, to me now — was a general castigation of the time in which he found himself, and a diatribe in especial against America, against the conditions of life and the democratic institutions of our land of freedom. Although his invective seemed to have no relation to life in America as I knew it, yet it went on for long reverberating beneath all the optimisms and enthusiasms and patriotic beliefs of my boyish years.

Thus to children at odd moments come, as through windows left unexpectedly ajar, intimations of the unknown aspects of the world they live in. In my grandfather's house there was another half-open window, through which I would sometimes peep with wondering eyes.

The life of the Quakers in Philadelphia, where we lived as children, was that of a secluded community, carefully entrenched and guarded from all contact with what we called the "World" — that dangerous world of wickedness which, we vaguely knew, lay all about us. With that world and its guilty splendors we had no contact; of the fashionable American aristocracy (and every population has its aristocracy and fashion) we were not members; and I can make no claim, as Americans abroad are apt to claim, that I belong to one of what are called America's first families. With members of this greater world, like Edith Wharton and Mrs. Winthrop Chanler, I became acquainted only after I had come to live in Europe.

No, we spent our youth amid the evangelical plainness and the simple ways of living of the stricter Philadelphia Friends. And yet,

those richly carved and velvet-covered chairs
which adorned my grandfather's drawing-
room at Germantown, those antlers which
hung on the walls of his suburban residence —
these seemed to tell a tale of richer experience,
and tinged for me with gayer colors the past
history and the European expeditions of the
old gentleman who sat reading upstairs.

The theme of the American abroad has
given rise to a considerable literature in recent
years; its earlier documents are less well
known, and it was with a good deal of interest
that I recently read my grandfather's account
of his experiences in Europe, and the authentic history of those trophies which had so impressed me as a boy. In my grandfather a
tendency, which he bequeathed to his descendants, manifested itself at an early date, to
make "jaunts," as he called them, to Europe;
and in 1845 he had gone to England on a sailing packet, accompanied by my father. On his
return he published in two volumes, under the
title of *A Summer's Jaunt across the Waters*,
an account of this journey. To boast of the

[18]

distinguished acquaintances they have made abroad is one of the most legitimate satisfactions of returned Americans, and this was plainly one of the motives which inspired the composition of my grandfather's volumes.

The Philadelphia Quakers had always kept up a connection with the members of their sect in England, and this connection was frequently renewed by the visits of English Friends on holy missions. Some of these visiting Friends belonged to the highest sphere of the Quaker world — for all religious communities, however holy, are stratified in social layers of increasing splendor — and the impressiveness of their doctrine was much augmented by a sense of the plain yet brilliant world in which they lived, a world of Barclays and Gurneys and other rich English Quaker families which, like a Quaker Versailles, holy and yet splendid, shone for us across the Atlantic with a kind of glory — a glory which, to tell the truth, has never completely faded from my eyes.

My grandfather, though not interested in

their doctrines, was by no means indifferent to the country houses and opulent tables of these English Quakers; he tells of dining with Samuel Gurney at Ham House, of meeting Elizabeth Fry, and of hearing her, in her feeble but honored old age, make a beautiful prayer from her large mahogany armchair in the meeting she attended. He tells also of being welcomed among a company of English Friends by a fellow Philadelphian and youthful acquaintance, Eliza P. Kirkbride, who had married, as his third wife, the eminent and opulent Joseph John Gurney.

But the great glory of this jaunt abroad of my grandfather was his visit to Stoke Park, then the residence of Granville Penn, William Penn's great-grandson and heir. Granville Penn, learning, according to my grandfather's account, — and I dare say by a note from my grandfather himself, — that a descendant of William Penn's secretary had come from Pennsylvania to England, sent him an invitation to Stoke Poges, which was accepted with alacrity. He relates how an elegant family carriage with liveried servants met him at the station; how he was conducted to the noble family mansion of the Penn family, where he spent some days, and in whose deer park he shot the buck of which the antlers afterwards adorned his suburban home; how his host drove him about the neighborhood in a coach with four horses, and took him to Oxford, where they dined at a raised table in the hall of Christ Church, and where, he tells with undisguised elation, all the guests except Mr. Penn and himself were lords.

These were indeed rich experiences; encouraged by them, my grandfather, five years after his return to America, started out on a still more glorious jaunt abroad. The great Crystal Palace Exhibition was then in preparation, and he had the happy idea of traveling to Europe as a sort of self-appointed and unofficial envoy to arrange, if possible, for the transport of this exhibition, or a portion of it, across the Atlantic after it had run its course in England. His purpose, as he states in his memoirs, was in part at least the utility to America of this plan, but his main intention, as he frankly admits, was to gain by this means "an introduction to men of mark abroad, and a sight of foreign life behind the scenes." Though the public part of his scheme came to no fruition, his private aim was brilliantly successful. Procuring a letter of recommendation from the Secretary of State at Washington, he proceeded to London, where he was received by Lord Granville and made the acquaintance of a certain General Gray, whom he describes as "a most elegant and portly gentleman." In London also he was privileged to witness the Duchess of Sutherland purchase a rug, which was indeed a sight of foreign life behind the scenes. He sat at tables, he tells his descendants, "of the most *recherché* character"; and once when the royal box at the Opera had been lent to someone of his acquaintance, and he was invited to share it, he had reason to believe, he tells us, that he was mistaken by some of the opera-goers for a foreign prince who was then on a visit to England.

Most "gratifying" of all his experiences

("gratifying" and "elegant" are favorite words in his vocabulary) was his reception by Queen Victoria's uncle, King Leopold, in Belgium. The King of the Belgians, who was much interested in the proposed London Exhibition, wished to discuss the project of its transference to America; but that thrifty monarch seems on this occasion to have done a good bit of business on his own account, since he induced my grandfather to purchase from a workshop of his own two expensive and elaborately carved chairs, facsimiles of the chair in which the King was wont to seat his own royal person. These splendid chairs, reeking with the bad taste of the Louis-Philippe period, my grandfather conveyed home with him in great triumph on the new steamer, the *Atlantic*, on which steamer one of the fellow passengers was the singer Jenny Lind, who "was most affable, and danced and sang the whole trip, the weather being admirable."

The echo of these glories, the sight of these antlers and royal chairs, must have seemed

evidences of a "gayness" they could not but
deplore to the stricter Quakers of Philadelphia, to whom my mother's family belonged,
and among whom my sisters and I spent our
childish years. But into the hearts of these
most unspotted of the Chosen People had not
the spirit of the world found an entrance,
though unsuspected by themselves? No
dreams, indeed, of dining with lords, of opera
boxes, or of being mistaken for foreign
princes, troubled, I am sure, their medita-
tions in their silent Meetings; but when some
opulent Friend from England came to preach
the gospel to them, was not the impressiveness of his or her doctrine tinged and deep-
ened by a sense of the sanctified splendor of
such English Friends? Had they not indeed
among them a living representative of that
splendor in the Eliza Kirkbride who had
reigned at Earlham, and with whom my
grandfather had dined in England, and who,
after the decease of her husband, — that
eminent evangelist, Joseph John Gurney, —
had returned to her native city, where,

[24]

preaching with great acceptance, she now reigned as a kind of Quaker queen, with many courtiers to listen to her holy boastings? Among these courtiers, one of the most assiduous was my mother's mother, Friend Mary Whitall, who was in our childhood always holding up before us the figure of Friend Gurney as the glass of Quaker fashion, and the very mould of form among the stricter Friends.

Thus into my boyish heart the spirit of the World found its entrance in various disguises, and intimations were also not wanting of those other enemies of our souls, the Flesh and the Devil.

It has become of late the fashion to speak with great frankness on sex matters, and many eminent authors dwell with especial emphasis on the first awakenings in them of a consciousness of this kind. Why should I not follow their example? These awakenings often come to innocent youth in troubled ways, and my first awareness of the allurements of what we call the Flesh was derived from circumstances of an unusual nature. Barnum's Circus came to Philadelphia in my boyhood, rousing considerable excitement in the youth of that quiet city; and among the Quakers the question was much debated whether their children should be allowed to witness this entertainment. While it was admitted on the one hand that the sight of the elephants and the other exotic animals would help to enhance their conception of the wonders of creation, there were grave fears on the other hand that the spectacle of the scantily clad female acrobats on the tightropes might sully the innocence of their childish minds. The compromise finally arrived at, at least in our family, was that the children should be taken to the circus and allowed to see the animals, but should sit with closed eyes while the acrobats were performing.

So there we sat, a row of Quaker children, staring with all our eyes at the performing elephants, but with our organs of vision closed and our hands before them during the less seemly interludes. But one little Quaker boy permitted himself a guilty peep through his fingers, and gazed on a show of muscular limbs moving, slowly moving, in pink tights. What he was gazing at was, he knew, the spectacle of Sin; and so striking was the impression that his concept of that word became colored in his imagination for a long time with the pinkness of those slowly moving legs. It was only long afterwards that he came to understand why he had been forbidden to gaze upon them, and the grave danger he might have thereby incurred.

While notions of the World and the Flesh reached me in hints that I hardly comprehended, I had no doubts about the Devil: his activities were present to my apprehension in visible forms, about which there could be no mistake. The godly community of Philadelphia Quakers, going their ways and attending to their affairs in peace and quietness, would, to an observer from outside, have seemed a uniform community of pious people, all dressed in the same garb, all speaking the same language, all living in the same houses, all sitting in the same meditative silence, or listening to the same doctrines in the same square, unadorned meetinghouses. To such a superficial observer, William Penn's ideal of brotherly love, which he had expressed in the name of the city he had founded, would indeed have seemed to have been realized among them. As a matter of fact, however, this pious folk was divided into two bitterly hostile races, each of which regarded the other with holy abhorrence. There were two sets of meetinghouses, two sets of burial places, two orders of preachers of the Quaker faith; and between the adherents of one sect and those of another no relations could ever occur. This gulf was the result of a doctrinal earthquake which early in the nineteenth century had shaken the foundations of Quakerism in America and split it into two bodies — the orthodox sect on one side of the gulf, who clung to the stricter Trinitarian theology, and on the other the followers of Elias Hicks. Elias Hicks seems to have been much more like one of the primitive Quakers than their respectable and orthodox successors. The decorums, or even ceremonies they had adopted as they grew in worldly prosperity, he rejected, along with the orthodox doctrines which had come to prevail among them. The true Christian religion, the old man preached (he lived to be nearly ninety), consisted in neither rites nor sermons nor Sundays, but in the love of God and of our neighbors, in the Inner Light, and the ideal aspirations of the soul. The blood of Christ which cleanses us from sin was, he declared, not His material blood. At the great Yearly Meeting of Philadelphia in which the schism originated, he made use of these words, "The blood of Christ — the blood of Christ, why, my friends, the actual blood of Christ in itself is no more effectual than the blood of bulls and goats — not a bit more, not a bit." These words were followed by a great tumult. Hundreds rose to their feet, canes were pounded on the floor. Many left the meeting, more remained with flushed faces and angry eyes. This was the definite beginning of the great split and separation — the yawning of that gulf which opened between the orthodox Quakers, who accepted the statement of the Bible, "It is the blood that maketh an atonement for the soul," and the followers of Elias Hicks, who took a more allegorical and therefore Socinian view. At the time of the division these two factions fought each other like Quaker demons, quarreling over their meetinghouses and burial places, and digging up their dead to save them from pollution, and these quarrels had left behind them a legacy of undying hate.

Both my father's and my mother's families were adherents of the orthodox or conservative party, and Hicksite Quakers were to my boyish apprehensions undoubtedly nothing less than children of the Devil. Even now, when I see my friend John Balderston, I shudder a little at the thought that though Samuel Kite, one of the most orthodox of the preachers in Germantown Meeting, was his grandfather, he himself played as a child with Hicksite boys in the street. But he was a bad

[30]

boy, I fear, from his birth, and that he should end up at Hollywood need not surprise us. I remember climbing the wall that surrounded one of the Hicksite meetinghouses, and gazing in on those precincts with all the horror of one who gazes into Hell. Never since have I looked upon any object with such feelings of abomination.

This theological horror was accompanied, among the orthodox at least, by an immense sense of social superiority: ours were the high places, we felt, in this world as well as in the next. This feeling that the Hicksites were outcasts and untouchables and social pariahs, though it had no foundation in fact, for they were as well off and as well-descended as we were, and probably a more enlightened and cultivated set of people — this sense of social superiority is the main religious feeling which I still retain; and even now, when, as sometimes happens, I meet in London Philadelphians with the taint in their veins of Hicksite blood, I seem to know them at once, as by a kind of instinct, by a subtly mingled sense of theological and social repugnance, which I find it extremely difficult to overcome.

My grandfather had married a Rachel Pearsall, of a Quaker family in Long Island, and my father, Robert Pearsall Smith, was, by his marriage in 1851 to my mother, Hannah Whitall, introduced into surroundings and circumstances different from those of his own family. His wife's father, John Whitall, was descended from another, more pious and less bookish line of New Jersey Quakers, being the grandson of that rather terrific Ann Whitall, of whose old religious journal I have written elsewhere. He had run away to sea as a boy, and, sailing before the mast on East Indian voyages, had become the captain of a merchantman at the age of twenty-four. On retiring from the sea he purchased a glass factory in New Jersey, and founded a manufacturing business which, owing to the admirable output of glass bottles, had prospered with the years, and indeed still prospers. My father, after several unsuccessful business adventures, had, owing to his marriage to my mother, been given a partnership in this firm.

My father was a man of fine presence, and of a sanguine, enthusiastic temperament, too impulsive to manage his own affairs by himself; however, being restrained by the caution of his cautious partners, his gifts of imagination were made to contribute to the firm's prosperity. He was, above all, a magnificent salesman; and traveling all over the United States, and offering the firm's wares to the chemists of the rapidly expanding Republic, he exercised upon those apothecaries the gifts of persuasion and blandishment, almost of hypnotization, which were destined later, in European and more exalted spheres, to produce some startling results. However, before he undertook these journeys, he had been placed for some years in charge of the glass factories in New Jersey; and it was in a small New Jersey town, with the romantic name of Millville, that I was born in 1865.

Unforgotten Years

My earliest recollections are tinged with the gleam of those great fiery furnaces which I used to gaze at from a distance. To my infant apprehensions the whole alarming picture, with the half-naked glass blowers moving like devils among the flames, presented a vivid image of what I believed might very likely be my future fate. For partly owing to the more serious religious tone of my mother's family, but still more (for the darker aspects of Christian doctrine were not much dwelt on by good Quakers) to the lava stream of evangelical revivalism into which my parents were swept away, the notion of Hell formed a fiery background to my childish thoughts; I was always expecting, half in terror, half in thrilled anticipation, to hear the blast of the Last Trumpet, to see the earth and heavens collapse and the sinners led off to their abodes of Eternal Torment.

The old doctrines of the corruption of man and his inevitable doom unless he finds salvation in the conviction of sin, the gift of grace, and a sudden catastrophic, miraculous conversion — this evangelical theology, though I was nourished on it in my youth, and tasted its joys and terrors, has now become utterly alien and strange to me. I cannot reconstruct in imagination that melodramatic world of hopes and terrors. I know, of course, that this body of convictions has an important place in religious history, and that, as a scheme of salvation, millions have fervently believed in it.

My parents, dissatisfied with what they considered the spiritual deadness of Quaker doctrine, welcomed the new outburst in America of revivalism, into which they plunged as into a great flood of life-giving water; and their evangelical activities formed for many years the absorbing interest of their lives. They went to revivalist meetings, they preached, they both wrote innumerable tracts, they converted souls, they lived in constant expectation of the Day of Judgment; and this highly colored world, with the heights of Heaven above them and the abysses of Hell beneath — this, and not their

[35]

commonplace and commercial surroundings, formed the environment in which they lived with such feverish excitement. We children naturally caught the infection of this excitement; and were encouraged to embark in our tender years upon these spiritual adventures.

There can be no doubt that I was born a vessel of wrath, full to the brim of that Original Sin we all inherit from that crude apple that diverted Eve. I was, as my mother's letters of the time bear witness, greedy, given to fits of temper, and, as she expressed it, a gorilla for screaming. Against this old Adam in me one of the kindest and the best of mothers strove with all her strength, but strove in vain. "Logan and I," she writes when I was four months old, "had our first regular battle to-day, and he came off conqueror, though I don't think he knew it. I whipped him till he was actually black and blue, and until I *could not* whip him any more, and he never gave up one single inch." In this state of sin I remained till I was four years old, when, however, I was rescued from it by my elder sister, now Mrs. Bernard Berenson, who, at the age of six, following the example of our parents, began the career of an evangelist, which she has since abandoned. I, who was then two years younger than herself, was the first object of her holy zeal. One memorable day she and a like-minded maiden named Fanny Potts led me to our bathroom, and there they prayed and wrestled with my carnal nature, until the great miracle of Conversion was accomplished in me.

"O Lord," prayed the future Mrs. Berenson, "please make little Logan a good boy; and don't let him tell any more lies!"

And then little Fanny Potts also lifted up her voice in prayer. "Lord, please give Logan a new heart."

Their prayer was granted, and a new heart was bestowed upon little Logan. But this heart, though purged of all former sin, was by no means immune from temptation in the future. He had in fact reached on this occasion the state of Justification only, not that of Sanctification, which, according to evangelical theology, renders us immune from sin. Again and again Satan would enter into his heart, and he would fall into sin again. In vain were his efforts to keep good by the force of his own will alone; and it was only after three years of spiritual struggle, lasting from the age of four to that of seven, that he renounced these Pelagian attempts to conquer Sin and Satan by his own carnal struggles, and realized that only by Grace, and unmerited Grace alone, and by no "deadly doing," could he attain the conquest that he sought.

All these facts I learn from a tract of my father's which I recently found among some old papers. The history of my struggle and salvation I had half forgotten, though I could still remember my infant agonies. This tract had an unusually large circulation, and, penetrating to the Western districts of America, made a powerful impression on the remaining tribes of Red Indians, who were converted

by it in their thousands. Such, at least, was
our family legend; and I remember the pride
I took in the conversions thus accomplished;
and believing, as I then believed, that each
of us should wear as stars in our diadems in
Heaven the souls which we had saved on
earth, I took a holy delight in the prospect
of shining in the courts of Heaven with the
radiance of these rubies of the West.

I sometimes wonder if the children I see
to-day playing about partake of the rich
experiences of my childhood. Do they feel
that they are disporting themselves on a thin
crust above the flames of Hell; and when
they are taken home do their mothers beat
them black and blue to drive out the old
Adam from within their tender skins? Do
they strive, as we used to strive, to keep out
Satan from their hearts, and pass their
young years tormented as I was by the grim
fact of sin and the dire necessity of grace?
If not, many pains are no doubt spared them,
but many joys and exaltations also. The
glorious certainty that they are sanctified

among millions doomed to Eternal Torment can never fill their hearts with holy pride, nor can they rejoice — as all my life I have rejoiced — in the consciousness that they can commit no wrong. I may do, I have undoubtedly done, things that were foolish, tactless and dishonest, and what the world would consider wrong, but since I attained the state of Sanctification at the age of seven I have never felt the slightest twinge of conscience, never experienced for one second the sense of sin.

2

First Visit to Europe

NOT LONG AFTER the memorable event of my conversion, our family went to Europe. My father's health had been affected by his combined mercantile and evangelical exertions; a period of rest and change was recommended by his doctors, and it was thought that this rest and change could be best procured in England. So in 1872 we embarked, my sisters and I, with our handsome florid father and our beautiful straightforward Quaker mother.

Both our parents were quite without any anticipation of the extraordinary experiences which awaited them. It is not my purpose to tell in any detail the story of these experiences. Let it suffice to say that news had already reached England of my father's gifts and successes as an evangelist; my mother's fame had also spread abroad, and when they arrived in London they were received with an interest which soon became enthusiasm, and finally almost a frenzy, in that strange world of evangelicals which was once so important, but which has now almost disappeared. It was a world, as I remember it, of large, opulent, ruddy aristocrats, living in great London mansions or country houses, and much given to immense collations and extempore prayers and the propagation of innumerable children. These personages often drove up to the house my father rented at Stoke Newington in the London suburbs, and my sisters and I would peep out through the windows at their fine carriages and horses, and would sometimes be presented to some large, friendly, red-faced man or woman whom we would be summoned to meet in the drawing-room. Often too, while our parents were rapt away to earnest conferences, we would be deposited in some country house, either with the Barclays at Monkhams in Essex (Mrs. Barclay was by birth one of the Gurneys of Earlham, and we thus became acquainted with the world of which we had heard so much from Friend Gurney in Philadelphia), or else at Broadlands in Hampshire, the home of our parents' friends, the Cowper Temples.

When our parents had first arrived in England, they had been invited to a drawing-room meeting of leading Evangelicals, which was summoned to judge whether their doctrine was perfectly sound according to the strictest standards. All was well save on one point, about which there were dreadful whispers. From something my mother had said or written, it had come to be suspected that she was not altogether sound on the doctrine of Eternal Torment.

Hell, it was known, she believed in, but did she hold that its torments were destined to endure forever? As a matter of fact, she did n't; and although my father and her friends besought her to conceal this heresy, when the crisis came and the question was put plainly to her in that London drawing-room, with that large company gravely waiting for her

[43]

answer, a sudden impulse came upon her to tell the truth. She knew that her own and perhaps her husband's career as expositors of the Gospel might be ruined by this avowal; she had agreed that it would be wiser to give evasive answers on this point; but she suddenly felt that if she was questioned she must say what she thought, whatever might be the consequences; and if she had been capable of using such a profane expression she would have told herself that she did n't care a damn.

She could not, she avowed to the assembled company, believe that the God she worshiped as a God of love was capable of such awful cruelty; sinners, of course, He punished, but that He had decreed that their torments should be unending was to her a horrible belief. Her auditors were inexpressibly dismayed by this declaration; the myrtle, in Keats's phrase, "sickened in a thousand wreaths"; the company was on the point of breaking up in confusion when from the depths of that great drawing-room there floated forward, swathed in rich Victorian draperies and laces, a tall and stately lady, who kissed my mother, and said, "My dear, I don't believe it either."

This dramatic moment was, perhaps, a turning point in my life, since, if it had not occurred, our family would no doubt have soon returned to America, and the ties and friendships which drew us all back again to England would never have been formed. For this lady who thus intervened and took my mother under her protection was, as it were, the queen of evangelical Christians; and her acceptance, afterwards confirmed by that of her husband, William Cowper Temple, silenced all opposition and no further objections were suggested.

The Cowper Temples, owing to their great wealth and high position, were by far the most important people in the world in which my parents were, so to speak, on trial. Cowper Temple was in law the son of Earl Cowper, but said to be the son of Lord Palmerston, who had long been Lady Cowper's friend, and who married her when Lord Cowper died.

Their son had inherited Lord Palmerston's estates and great house at Broadlands; and the problem of this double paternity, if I may put it so, which was the gossip of the time (gossip which sounded strangely in our Philadelphian ears), had been successfully regulated by the young William Cowper's adding Lord Palmerston's family name of Temple to that of Cowper in a double appellation. After acting as secretary to his unavowed father, he served in several posts in the governments of the time and was raised to the peerage as Lord Mount Temple in 1880. His wife, who had corroborated my mother's view of Hell, is known in the history of art as the friend of the Pre-Raphaelites, and above all as the Egeria of Ruskin, who describes in his *Praeterita* how, when in Rome in 1840, he had first seen the beautiful Miss Tollemache (as she was then), and how, though he never met her, he had haunted the Roman churches on the chance of catching a glimpse of her sweet and statuesque beauty — a kind of beauty which had hitherto been only a dream to him — and

[46]

how the thought of seeing her, if but in the distance, became, he tells us, the hope and solace of his Roman sojourn. It was only fourteen years later that he was introduced to her in London and became her friend.

Her friendship with my mother lasted till her death in extreme old age. She became a beautiful old saint, in whose character my mother could find only one flaw, if flaw it could indeed be called. Lady Mount Temple could never grasp the difference between right and wrong; when no cruelty was involved she could n't see why people should not do what they liked. My mother would try to explain moral distinctions to her, and though Lady Mount Temple would say at the moment that she understood them, they soon faded from her mind.

When Oscar Wilde was out on bail between his two trials, she wrote him a friendly letter, inviting him to pay her a visit, by which letter, Oscar Wilde tells us, he was greatly touched. Her family, the Tollemaches, were a wild family, much given to misbehavior, and

[47]

when one or another got in disgrace she would invite the offender to her home and would often send for my mother, as one familiar with right and wrong, to come and help the erring one back to the righteous path. I remember my mother's telling of one occasion when a Tollemache, married to a foreign prince, had run away from him with a lover, and then had been placed under Lady Mount Temple's roof to be made to realize the impropriety of her conduct. My mother was as usual summoned, and arrived in her Quaker garb and with her Bible, to help in this work of moral reformation. The Bible was read, there were prayers and exhortations, and all seemed to be going on in a most satisfactory manner, till one day, entering the old lady's writing room, my mother noticed that she was trying to conceal a piece of paper, and, when questioned, she confessed that she was composing a telegram for the lover of the erring lady to come and join them, since, as she put it, she felt that Matilda was feeling so lonely without him.

First Visit to Europe

In her old age, Lady Mount Temple fell under the almost intolerable domination of a pious cook, and my mother was appealed to by the family to try to free her from this tyrant. But when my mother informed her of the fact (which she had ascertained) that this holy woman was the mother of a large family of illegitimate children, the only answer she received was, "My dear, I am so glad poor Sarah has had some fun." My mother, seeing that a charge of misconduct made no impression, thereupon visited the eldest of this irregular family, and suggested to him that as his mother must have saved a large sum of money, it might be wise to remove her to his home, and thus probably inherit her savings when she died. The son saw the wisdom of this suggestion, and Lady Mount Temple was made free at last.

But all this happened years after the occasion of which I have been writing, on which occasion we were promptly invited to come to Broadlands, whither we soon proceeded, my mother, my father, my two sisters, and myself. Broadlands became thenceforward almost our home in England, and in its ample halls were gathered innumerable guests, to listen to the glad tidings of salvation which had reached the shores of England from across the Atlantic Ocean.

My mother and father had more than once attended camp meetings in America, where, amid primeval forests or by the shore of some mountain lake, evangelicals had been accustomed to gather for holy jubilations (not always unaccompanied by hysterical outbursts in which the Chosen People would scream and dance and roll upon the earth); and as they often described to their hosts these outpourings of the spirit, it occurred to the good Cowper Temples to inaugurate a series of such meetings in their park upon the banks of the Test in England, and this project was successfully carried out. My father was an acceptable preacher at these meetings; but my sincere simple-minded mother, beautiful in her Quaker dress, with her candid gaze and golden hair, was given the name of "the Angel of the Churches," and her expositions of the Gospels, delivered in the great beautiful eighteenth-century orangery in the Park at Broadlands, attracted the largest audiences, and made those gatherings famous in the religious world.

They were unattended, however, by any of the wilder phenomena of the American camp meetings, with which my mother had no sympathy, and I cannot recall the spectacle of any English aristocrats foaming at the mouth or rolling in holy ecstasy upon those Hampshire lawns.

It is odd to me now to reflect that while these meetings were going on at Broadlands, quite possibly Dante Gabriel Rossetti was also in the house in person (while in spirit such immeasurable miles away), for he often, I believe, stayed at Broadlands, and painted some of his pictures and wrote some of his poems there. But on us, if we saw him (and we may have seen him), he made, and could have made, no impression at all.

The beauty of Broadlands, with its park and shining river and the great house, full of history and portraits, and crowded with eminent people earnestly seeking Salvation for their souls, had a great effect upon my childish imagination; and when I now recall this period of our lives I cannot but regard as a fantastic adventure this sudden transference of a family of plain-living, middle-class Philadelphia Quakers into circumstances and surroundings so different from what they had been accustomed to. As a proud little American boy, I treasured up at Broadlands boasts with which to impress the boys at home; I remember especially the glory of one week, when there was a horse show in Broadlands park, and a special box was provided for the Cowper Temples and their guests. They were too busy of course in their search for Salvation to occupy this box, but I loved to sit there all by myself, in the gaze of the whole assembled county, with my little heart almost bursting, even at that early age, with emotions for which the word "snobbish" is, I fear, the only appropriate name. But there were humiliations, as well as glories, for an American boy in those great houses — above all the wise exclusion of children from the evening dinners, an exclusion unheard of in our American world. When, on our first visit to the Barclays at Monkhams, I was summoned to supper with the Barclay children in the nursery, I bitterly declined the invitation; said I had no appetite, and sat weeping in hungry pride in my bedroom. In the stately halls of Broadlands there was no such interdict; my elder sister dressed herself up as a young lady and went in to dinner with the rest, but in the crowd of guests I was occasionally overlooked; and I remember one occasion, almost worthy of a page in Proust, when the stately procession swept along to the dining room, and I was left behind. My little heart was full of bitterness and my eyes of tears, when the Duchess of Sutherland, a Duchess famous for her beauty, who had noticed my plight as she passed me, considerately left the dining room and returned and took me by the hand and arranged a seat for me at her side. I should like to think that this was the same Duchess of Sutherland whom my grandfather, in his anxiety for a sight of foreign life behind the scenes, had seen purchasing a rug so many years before. I am afraid, however, that chronology forbids.

There are few human beings more detestable to me than spoiled American children, who, full of their own importance, demand continual attention, and are the ruin of all rational talk among grown-up people. But my hatred of these noisy little monsters is — or at least it ought to be — tempered by the recollection that I was in my childhood one of them myself, and must have been at Broadlands a nuisance, which my American parents would, of course, have done nothing to abate.

That the five of us, my father, my mother, my two sisters, and myself, should be invited to stay for weeks and even months in these English country houses gives one an enlarged conception of the hospitality of those times. We children shared governesses with the

[54]

immense populations of their nurseries, and sometimes attended little local schools in their company. The boys of my own age were naturally my companions; they were for the most part Etonians. Anyone seeking for the home of unspotted purity would probably not pause in his search at an English public school; but the behavior and conversation of these polite Etonians, though they would have interested Proust, could not have been expected to reveal to the holy little Samuel of Philadelphia anything that was not innocent and pure. I remember one of these boys taking me up into a walnut tree in his father's park, and treating me to a display which, though it had no interest for me at the time, yet I felt, as a mark of friendliness from an English to an American boy, was a demonstration of international good will.

My mother paid little attention to all the unaccustomed circumstances in which she found herself at Broadlands; those to whom

she preached were in her eyes little more than
souls she hoped she could help to a true knowledge of the gospel truths; but my father was
immensely delighted by his sanctified success
among the great ones of this earth. If his
head was turned by it, one can hardly blame
him; though a little worldly wisdom (but
what chance had he ever had of acquiring
worldly wisdom?) might have given him
some notion of the fantastic character of this
adventure. Even the presence at Broadlands
of a large black evangelical negress from
America, named Amanda Smith, who would
also expound the Scriptures to the earnest
but indiscriminating ears of the assembled
company — even the concurrence of this
holy negress (whom my mother came to like
and made a friend of) and the necessity of
sharing his triumphs with this dusky rival,
though no doubt extremely repugnant to
him, did not in the least warn my father of
the sandy basis upon which his fairy castle
was being built. Indeed, as its airy pinnacles
rose higher and higher in the sky, he became

incapable of listening to the warnings my mother gave him of the risks he ran.

How could he listen? Ruddy, handsome, with the fine whiskers so admired at that date, rich from the proceeds of the bottle factory at home, and, unlike other evangelists, paying his own way in a lordly fashion, he became, as his fame spread from Broadlands, more or less the rage in religious circles. His photograph adorned the windows of the London shops; immense crowds flocked to his ministrations; his thrilling voice held audiences of thousands in rapt attention. Soon his reputation as a preacher crossed the Channel; he was invited to Paris, where he held many meetings; the wives of monarchs in Belgium and Holland welcomed him to those countries, and discussed the state of their royal souls with him in private interviews. In the churches thousands listened spellbound to the doctrines he proclaimed. I have already spoken of the two steps of my conversion, the first that of Justification, by which all my sins committed in the past were washed

[57]

away, and the second step, that of Sanctification, which rendered me immune to sin in
the future. The doctrine of the separation, as
by different operations of the Spirit, between
Justification and Sanctification was widely
held by the Wesleyans, who found much
authority for it, they thought, in the Scriptures. It was very prevalent in America
when my father began to preach it to the
"miserable sinners" of England. To believe
that, by an act of faith, they had become
"dead to sin," as Saint Paul expressed it, was
received as the most glorious of good tidings.
Proclaimed first by my father in 1873, and
then at Broadlands, it was decided to hold
a great meeting at Oxford in the autumn of
1874, and the university city was filled with
earnest Christians of almost all denomina-
tions, and many ecclesiastical dignitaries.
Professor Warfield of Princeton has published, under the title of *Perfectionism* (Oxford Press, 1931), an admirable and scholarly
account of the whole movement, and the
part played in it by my father. The effect of

[58]

the Oxford meeting was, he says, nothing
less than amazing. Many foreign as well as
English Christians were assembled there, and,
above all, German theologians, who insisted
that my father should come and proclaim the
good news to that country. To Germany he
went, therefore, in 1875, where he met with
an almost royal reception. The Emperor lent
him a church, he was granted an interview
with the Empress Augusta, and the most distinguished theologians attended his sermons.
My father knew no German, but the necessity
of translation seemed only to increase his
evangelical power. The old Pietist associations were revived, and the divine glow
seemed to illuminate all Germany, where a
religious sect was formed which, I am told,
still exists with thousands of adherents.

To England my father returned for further
triumphs. "There is nothing more dramatic
in the history of modern Christianity," Professor Warfield writes, "than the record of
this 'Higher Life' Movement," as it was
called. Brighton was occupied with even

more earnest Christians than was Oxford,
more church dignitaries, and more famous
foreign preachers; the Dome was filled to
overflowing, and the sermons had to be repeated in the Corn Exchange. "All Europe is
at my feet," Professor Warfield records my
poor father as exclaiming when he stood on
the platform of the Dome. But almost immediately an announcement appeared in the
papers that he had been compelled to cancel
all his engagements and to return almost at
once to America. It was suggested that a fall
from a horse some years before had led to the
return of certain distressing symptoms which
rendered absolute rest necessary. I must say
that in the family we did n't believe in that
horse; at least I am certain that my mother
did n't. I don't think she ever referred to it
at all, which made people suspicious, and so
universal became the gossip that my father's
friends felt it necessary to issue a further explanation. It had come to their ears, they
stated, that my father had inculcated doctrines that were most dangerous and unscrip-

tural, and that there had been conduct on his part which, though it was free, they were convinced, from all evil intention, had rendered it necessary for him to abstain from public work, and take the complete rest rendered necessary by the fall from his horse. That the doctrine of Sanctification and Deadness to Sin might lead to dangerous forms of Antinomianism was well known from the history of the past; whether it was an unscriptural doctrine has been much discussed by theologians. But this was not the doctrinal quadruped from which my father slipped at Brighton. It was a much more mysterious beast which he had also brought from America, so mysterious that even the learned and profound Professor Warfield seems never to have guessed at its existence. But my mother knew it well; she was constantly warning my father against it, and in her old age she wrote a book to tell the world of its dreadfully dangerous character (*Religious Fanaticism*, Faber and Gwyer, 1928 [1]). So

[1] Reprinted in 1934 by Faber & Faber under the title of *Group Movements of the Past*, with a preface by the Bishop of Durham.

strongly was she convinced of its prevalence that she said there ought to be a preacher stationed on the top of every steeple, to warn Christian worshipers against it.

What exactly was the nature of this doctrine? I cannot find that it has a name, so for convenience I shall call it the doctrine of "Loving-kindness." It is one of the most ancient of heresies; it seems to have existed from the beginning of Christianity, and it is based moreover on a sound psychological basis — on the fact, namely, that nature, in one of her grossest economies, has placed the seats of spiritual and amorous rapture so close to each other that one of them is very likely to arouse the other. Even the holiest of saints and most devoted of nuns — so exactly do these two forms of ecstasy feel alike — have sometimes found it extremely difficult to distinguish between them. From this fact it was only too easy to form the heretical belief that this heightening of religious experience, due to the mingling of the sexes, was God's own way (and His ways

were mysterious and not to be questioned by
carnal reason) of bestowing His blessing
upon them. When a holy preacher sat near
a sanctified sister, or a female penitent close
to her confessor, they became more conscious of the Baptism of the Spirit; and, as
my mother sardonically expressed it, the
nearer to each other they sat, the deeper
and richer this consciousness became. To
describe this experience in carnal terms, indeed in any spoken words, was impossible;
it could only find expression in holy endearments. That the love feasts of the early Christians were followed by such endearments
was the universal view of the most enlightened pagans: we should recoil with horror,
Gibbon says, from such a notion, did not the
documents show that every sect of Christians
brought this accusation against every other
sect.

"Salute one another with a holy kiss,"
Paul enjoined upon the Romans; and it has
taken Christianity centuries to eliminate
from its proceedings this holy kiss — if in-

deed it has succeeded in doing so completely. Certainly in my father's time this exquisite, secret doctrine was extremely prevalent in America; and my father, in spite of my mother's almost desperate warnings, would expound it to select gatherings mostly composed of spinsters of a certain age. Unluckily one of these grew jealous of another, and let the great beautiful cat out of the bag, to the scandal of the righteous, and the extreme joy of the unholy, whose jokes about the "Higher Life," as it was called, made my father feel that it would be wise for him to cease his ministrations.

My mother naturally speaks harshly of this cat, which had brought such trouble into her life and that of so many of her friends. Whether this grimalkin has again pussyfooted its way across the Atlantic, and is playing its pranks among certain groups of earnest Christians, I cannot say.

As people grow old, it becomes very hard for them to keep clear in their minds the important distinction between Right and

[64]

Wrong — outlines become dim and one thing fades into another. Certainly it is extremely difficult, especially for her unsanctified descendants, not to detect a touch of amusement in my mother's book; a kind of — what shall I call it? — well, a kind of holy fun in her descriptions of the pranks played by this amazing animal in the abodes of the "dear, deluded saints," as she calls them, who made it their pet.

At the time, however, my father found it wise, as I have said, to cease his ministrations; though to the Cowper Temples, I think, — certainly to Mrs. Cowper Temple, — all this fuss seemed incomprehensible and silly. If these good people wanted to kiss each other, what, she wondered, could be the harm in that?

In sackcloth and ashes my father recrossed the Atlantic, not, like his father, with song and dancing; no staghorns, no royal chairs, were among his luggage. However, — and these coincidences are perhaps worth noting, — my mother brought with her a haunch of

venison from Dunrobin Castle, where she had
been on a visit, which haunch, given her by
the Duke of Sutherland, was consumed immediately on our return to Philadelphia by
ourselves and our relations with more snobbish than gastronomical delight.

The toughness, the lack of savor, of this
ducal haunch still linger on my palate, as my
first taste — there have been others — of the
vanity and insipidity of worldly things.

Then we settled down again in our Philadelphia suburb. In August 1876, Dr. Cullis
of Boston, a friend and fellow evangelist of
my father's, determined to get up a great
meeting to reinstate in the eyes of the Church
and the world this preacher whose reputation had been somewhat damaged by gossip
from England. Neither my father nor my
mother wanted this "scamp meeting," as
Dr. Cullis wittily called it, but he said "it
was of the Lord," and forced them to attend
it. They both hated, my mother writes to a
friend, the whole performance, and had no be-

lief in it. The meetings were a bore; the work, my mother writes, was like a treadmill, and they counted the hours till it should be over; "and all pious chroniclers," she adds, "and church historians would have been compelled by the force of Christian logic to have added to this record 'and no wonder the meeting was an utter failure.' But to give a plain, unvarnished statement of fact, I am compelled to add that the meeting was a perfect success. There was just the same power and blessing as at Oxford, and every sign of the presence of the Spirit. Souls were converted, backsliders restored, Christians sanctified, and all present seemed to receive definite blessings. And it really was a good meeting, even I, uninterested as I was, could see that. There was just the same apparent wave of blessing as swept over our English meetings. And Robert and I never worked more effectually. He had all his old power in preaching and leading meetings, and the self-same *atmosphere* of the spirit. As for me, thee knows I am not much given to tell of my own successes, but in this case, in order that thee may have all the *facts*, I shall have to tell thee that I was decidedly 'favoured,' as Friends say. And the fuss made over me was a little more than even in England. The preachers fairly sat at my feet, figuratively speaking, and *constantly* there kept coming to me testimonies of definite blessings received while I spoke. The second time I spoke a Democratic editor was converted and consecrated on the spot; and I could scarcely get a minute to myself for the enquirers who fairly overwhelmed me.

"And now what does thee think of it all? I think one of two things. But which one I think I don't know. Perhaps thee can tell me. Either I am awfully wicked in the whole matter, and God was not in it anywhere, and all the success was by natural gifts and talents. Or else I was awfully good, so good as to have lost sight of self to such a degree as to be only a straw wafted on the wings of the Spirit, and so consecrated as not to be able to form a desire even, except that the will of God might be fully done. I waver about myself continually. Sometimes I feel that I have progressed wonderfully, and that my present sphinx-like calm and indifference to everything whether inward or outward except the will of God is very grand. And then again I think I am utterly irreligious and a lazy fatalist, with not a spark of the divine in me. I do wish I could find out *which* I am. But at all events my *orthodoxy* has fled to the winds. I am Broad, Broader, Broadest!"

After this "scamp meeting," and the disillusion it brought, in spite of its success, my father became more sympathetic to my grandfather's want of faith; and this feeling was much increased by the daily companionship of his brother Lloyd, with whom he used to drive every morning behind a fine pair of horses (my father had a passion for fine horses) to the not distant city of Philadelphia.

I wish I knew more of this uncle of mine, Lloyd Pearsall Smith. I remember the abstracted look of his bookish eyes in his handsome face; I remember his distantly polite manner with his nieces and nephews, whom he faintly recognized, but whose names he could seldom remember; and I was allowed to visit the library over which, in succession to his father, he now presided with much dignity. The *Dictionary of American Biography* informs me that he was regarded as a most scholarly man and as better acquainted with library management than anyone else of his time. I imagine him as a disappointed, somewhat tragic figure, a true Smith of our line of Smiths, an immense reader and a writer, but without talent, to whom had never been vouchsafed any glorious jaunt across the Atlantic. His life had been broken, so gossip said, by an unhappy passion from which he had never recovered; he shared in none of the optimisms and beliefs of our little community, and I remember only one expression of his feelings, when he too, like my grandfather, opened his usually silent lips to a condemnation of America, and of the age he lived in — a condemnation more quietly expressed but much more bitterly contemptuous, and founded on a far more desolating analysis, than my grandfather's outburst, which had sounded so strangely in my ears.

Of an older brother of these two, named Albanus Smith, who died in his twentieth year in 1843, I have just found a pathetic little memoir, privately printed at his death. This forgotten uncle of mine, whose name I never heard of in my youth, was plainly one of our race of bookish spirits, who had heard from across the Atlantic the voices of the Muses, and wished also, though in vain, to become a man of letters like myself. Like me, he made an anthology of seventeenth-century writers, but his compilation of fine prose was never printed, and after a passionate recital of "Mazeppa" before a society of like-minded youths, he fell ill and died. He now joins for me that family group of dim and thwarted ghosts whose wishes and literary ambitions never found, as mine have found, some slightly more fortunate fulfillment. This uncle made a most pious, Christian, edifying end; some semblance of such a decease had been hastily improvised for my grandfather by my religious aunt with whom he lived; but when my other uncle died, it was not possible to improvise for him an edifying departure. He took his disbelief with him to the grave, and with it the secret of his thwarted life; and, as I was destined to a brighter career in the world of glittering glass bottles, the vacant and, as we fondly boasted, hereditary librarianship was filled by a stranger.

My father in the meantime, discussing, as I have said, the dark perplexities of religion as he drove daily with this irreligious brother to and from his office, had begun to lose his faith in the whole scheme of Salvation which he had so fervently advocated, and by means of which he had converted so many thousands of earnest souls. His situation was thus an awkward one; he had still a reputation in the religious world, he still possessed the hypnotic power of swaying great audiences, and many calls were made upon him to address meetings and administer religious instruction to souls in trouble. Invitations to preach he could avoid on the grounds of health, but the religious inquirers who called at the house, coming sometimes as far as from Russia, were the source of greater embarrassment; and I remember how desperately he would try to keep one or the other of his children in the room to avoid the necessity of a spiritual dialogue, and how quite heartlessly we would escape from it, leaving him to grapple alone with these spiritual inquirers. This we thought great fun.

Perhaps unconsciously affected by my father's loss of faith, or because the good seed in my case had fallen on extremely shallow ground, my early religious feelings began before long to fade away. They had remained with me for some years after my conversion, which had transformed me into an infant evangelist who would distribute religious tracts in the Philadelphia horsecars, and who, profoundly impressed by the necessity of doing something each day before the sun went down to save some human soul, would often hurry out towards evening to perform this godly task before it was too late. This zeal was maintained during our sojourn in England, and indeed increased by the holy excitement of that period; and I recall in especial one hot summer day, when, driving with my parents across the Isle of Wight, I was filled with an ineffable consciousness of Sanctification and exemption from the fear of Hell and the fate of others, which filled my little heart with a sensation of felicitous vanity more exquisite than any I have experienced since. The scent and taste of ripe peaches plucked from a sunny wall in August? No, I have felt nothing in my life which I can compare with that holy joy.

Leslie Stephen, in his essay on Jonathan Edwards, mentions the story, so similar to my own, of the redemption of little Phebe Bartlet, of Northampton, Massachusetts, who was, like me, converted at the age of four, and also made efforts to save the souls of others. The account of Phebe he describes as "the grotesque story of this detestable infant," or words to that effect. Such a detestable infant I must have been, no doubt; yet I was, after all, no Phebe Bartlet, but a healthy schoolboy; and the usual schoolboy interests and occupations began to fill my mind with more seasonable thoughts. Finally, one Sunday afternoon in June, when I was up in a cherry tree picking cherries, the whole supernatural scheme of things seemed to fade away into the blue sky, never to return.

Our summer holidays from school came more and more to be spent, as we grew older, in camping expeditions, first in the Adirondacks, or the Maine forests, and then amid the Rocky or the Californian mountains; and these delightful fishing and shooting trips, though they stored my mind with infinite forest and mountain memories which are still vivid and delightful, aroused in me a passion for wild life in the open air which obliterated not only my religious sentiments, but also my early taste for reading, and retarded whatever tendency there was in me towards the development of my mind. I became in my school days nothing more than an ordinary healthy boy, fond of games and sports, and above all of camping trips and fishing and shooting among wild lakes and mountains.

Not long ago, when I was reading Turgenev's *Sportsman's Sketches*, the memory came back of these old hunting days in the Rocky Mountains, the delicious fatigue felt through all the body on my return to camp with the game I had shot or the trout I had fished for (for I was game purveyor to the camp), and the nights spent in the open on pine boughs in the cool night wind, under the mountain stars. Then the dawns of those long-ago days brightened for me, and I remembered the preparations for another day of shooting, the proceeding forth with my rifle, the climbs and scrambles through virgin forests, the excitement and hush of the unseen presence of deer or elk or bear, then the heat and thirst in the midday sun, and the finding of bubbling streams among the mountains and the slaking of my overpowering thirst.

First Visit to Europe

When we were not on camping expeditions, we often went to Newport — not to the fashionable part of that fashionable watering place, but to the town on the harbor, where my uncle, James Whitall, and several Philadelphia Quakers owned old-fashioned houses, in which their summers were quietly spent; and memories of these sojourns amid a band of happy cousins often return to me now, and fill the background of my mind: the sailing in little boats, the sounds of guitars and youthful voices, the wind on starlit nights and the splash of the dark waters; the sight of the great steamers that passed like furnaces of light, and my departure at last in one of them, watching with tears and smiles the lanterns waved by cousins and friends from my uncle's wharf. To tuck a happy childhood under a child's jacket was the principle which my mother's kindly father often preached as the best preparation for happiness in future years, and such a childhood was certainly the provision which was made for us, adding greatly to the future felicity of our lives.

3

Walt Whitman

FROM THE Quaker Penn Charter School in Philadelphia I went at the age of sixteen to the near-by Quaker college at Haverford, and began to undergo that vague, diffused kind of intellectual varnishing and plastering over which was then regarded in the United States, and is, I believe, still regarded, as an adequate collegiate education. The scheme of teaching in this small Quaker college, though rather sounder, I believe, than that in some of the larger universities, had but little influence on me: no stirring of the mind resulted from those instructions; I played games; I spent my summers in shooting and fishing expeditions; I and my companions were simply enjoying our brief, irresponsible hour in the sun, before we should all take up that business career to which we were destined. That every American should make money, that even those who already possessed it should devote their lives to making more, that all of them without exception should betake themselves every morning to their offices and spend all the hours of sunlight in these great business buildings — this was the universally accepted and grotesque ideal of life in the world we lived in. We were, it is true, for the most part Quakers, but the unworldliness of this unworldly sect had not long been able to curb the pecuniary ardor which had soon taken possession of its members; and although my mother's father, the original founder of the family business, had put before himself a modest measure of permissible gain — limiting his ideal to the maintenance of a house in town and a house in the country, and a carriage and a pair of fat horses for his wife — and, when this had been attained, had religiously resigned all further profits to his partners, no such scruples troubled his successors in the business. As this business was now growing in importance and prosperity, glass furnace being added to furnace, and the output of glass bottles greatly increasing year by year, while my father drew an ever-increasing income from this source, it was taken for granted that I, his only surviving son, should, when the time came for him to retire, succeed him in this lucrative occupation. It was a golden chance and a dazzling prospect that quite obliterated all thought of the librarianship, with its meagre income, to which I had been originally destined.

In the meantime, raw college boy as I was, absorbed in outdoor sports, and glass manufacturer as I hoped to be in the future, I became nevertheless dimly conscious of certain vague stirrings in what, for want of a better term, I must call my mind. Haverford College had been built in a pleasant rural situation, with slopes and hills and a little lake, and many groves of trees. Amid one of these groves a little college library had been placed. I began to haunt this rustic and almost unfrequented little building; and the love of reading, early awakened in me by my visits to the old library in Philadelphia, began to take hold of me again.

And then, as I passed beyond the years of childhood, another impulse stirred within me, and contributed its energy to the dim awakening of my intellectual life. I became vaguely aware of Culture, not indeed as a thing of value in itself, but as bestowing a kind of distinction upon its possessors, a distinction superior in some mysterious way to that of a big-game killer which had hitherto been my ambition and my dream. The revelation to me of this ideal I owed to that elder sister who had converted me in my boyhood, and in whose footsteps, as she climbed one height after another, I followed with clumsy feet for many years.

Young American women, before they settle down to domestic felicity, permit themselves, and by the custom of the country are permitted, an unreproved period of fascination, a prenuptial flight as it were, on which they are pursued by such swarms as they can provoke — and they are allowed almost every license in provoking them — of admirers, suitors, beaux, and would-be lovers. This subjugation, this victimization and leading captive of susceptible young males, is — or at least was — the privilege and indeed the glory of every attractive young American female; and is, as I have said, a kind of prenuptial flight less dangerous after all than that of bees, for the hearts of the rejected in that sphere, though easily broken, are not difficult to mend, and the chosen mate or husband is not deprived of life when he has performed his duty to the race.

My sister had now begun to soar upward on shining pinions, followed by an unusual train of male admirers (for she was a great beauty), and it was into high realms of poetry and culture that she winged her flight. Thus to me, seated on the dull earth, there began to echo downward, as from a heaven of larks above, the most fascinating talk of literature and poetry. Oh, I thought, to be initiated into those refinements, to have read the right books, to be able to quote the fashionable poets, to shine, like my sister's admirers, in literary conversation! Was it possible that I, too, might one day learn to take my part in the discourse of these exalted regions? I shyly began to ask my sister about books, and she recommended me to read the fashionable prophets of the day, Carlyle and Emerson and Ruskin. These I found in the little college library among the trees, and I turned over their pages as if they were books of magic, from which some intimations of their real meaning began slowly to dawn upon me. The rhetoric of *Sartor Resartus* awoke in me a dim sense that my soul was somehow in a prison, and in Emerson's pages I caught faint glimpses of the free and starry life which might be possible to the emancipated spirit. Most potent of all was the influence of Ruskin upon me, and I remember in especial one vivid moment, when, lying out of doors in the grass one late summer afternoon, reading in *Modern Painters* about the clouds, I happened to look up from my book and saw above me the blue sky and the golden architecture of the unmoving summer clouds. I had seen many beautiful landscapes on my shooting and fishing expeditions; but this moment, when I gazed up at the sky and drank in its beauty, I have been wont to regard as my first experience of conscious æsthetic enjoyment. The dispositions, however, of which we become more aware as we grow older are deeply implanted in us, and are, indeed, part of our native endowment; and the other day, in reading a letter written by my mother before I was three years old, I found that she had noted at that early age how no object that pleased my eyes, no flower or autumn leaf or gay bit of rag, escaped my attention, and how "the perverse little mortal," as she described me, loved to sit and gaze up at bright-colored clouds. "I wish they would come down here," she once heard me exclaim, "and let me see how pink they are. I want," the pious infant added, "to show them to Jesus."

Soon after my reading of Ruskin I began to ask my sister about poetry and the poets.

Poetry, I had always maintained, was all rot
and nonsense, but I had become dimly aware
of the part it played in that exchange of sentiments and gallantries which was the main
interest and the great romantic preoccupation
of the youth of our community. This part was
indeed important; the flights of the young
females and their adorers were musical with
song; it was with the strains of the fashionable
poets, of Tennyson and Longfellow and Swinburne and the Brownings, on their lips that
the pursued and the pursuers soared upward
into the blue; and my sister, who was foremost
in these things among her aspiring companions, was accustomed to make the most effective use of this method of fascination. She
knew the whole of *In Memoriam* by heart; she
could chant pages of Swinburne and Mrs.
Browning by the hour, which she says she still
cannot forget; but there were certain poems
of Poe which were perhaps her favorites, and
her singing of "Annabel Lee" in the twilight
to soft piano accompaniment was well known
to be extraordinarily effective.

But our love it was stronger by far than the love
Of those who were older than we —
Of many far wiser than we —
And neither the angels in heaven above,
Nor the demons down under the sea,
Can ever dissever my soul from the soul
Of the beautiful Annabel Lee.

The sound of these strains faintly reaching our ears long ago was a warning to us all of the presence in the drawing-room of some youth to whom "Annabel Lee" thus sung in the twilight was almost invariably fatal. We took it as a warning that we must certainly not intrude. How far away and innocent seems to me now that way of life in our Philadelphia suburb — the thoughts we thought, the songs we sang, the things we talked about in our ugly house, with its imitation stained-glass windows and Landseer engravings!

However, to resume my tale. I had by this time become dimly aware of the prestige to be acquired by some knowledge of the poets, and by the ability to pronounce their names in a knowing way and to murmur their musical lines in the moonlight, and I began, in my conversations with my sister, to introduce shyly, as I have said, the subject of poetry. Yes, there was poetry, my sister answered, musing, and smiling to herself as she mused; and then with a pitying consciousness of my rudimentary culture, and a feeling, no doubt, that I was unworthy as yet of the higher initiations, — that Tennyson and Swinburne and Browning were still far beyond my scope, — she recommended me to read Macaulay's *Lays*, which I did read in the little library among the trees on my return to college — read with real excitement, although I hardly found in these heroic lays many tender lines suitable for quotation in the moonlight. More to my purpose was another book of poems which I found for myself upon those shelves, — Owen Meredith's *Lucile*, — which shoddy stuff I read with passion, finding in it the delineation of all that I thought most elegant and distinguished, all that in my most romantic moods I should have liked to be.

In the meantime, however, almost unknown to me, or vaguely apprehended, something had happened in another branch of my maternal family which, though I had at the time no notion of it, was destined to have a decisive effect upon my fate and fortunes. My mother's youngest sister had married a Baltimore physician; they were the parents of nine children, and in the eldest of these peculiar symptoms were beginning to alarm her family. This daughter had made friends with another Baltimore young girl, in whose house they had discovered and read with rapture the writings of a poet called by the name, hitherto unknown to them, of Shelley; Shelley had led them on to Godwin, whose writings they had also unearthed. They had adopted with enthusiasm all the doctrines of these two writers, their atheism, their belief in Free Love (exactly what Free Love was these maidens hardly knew, but they believed in it with passion); and my cousin, thus aware of larger horizons, had made up her mind to wider explorations of this intellectual world.

She had determined, in fact, to achieve a college education, which was then for women most unusual in America, and quite unheard of in our Quaker world. After a terrific struggle she made her way to Cornell University, one of the few colleges then open to women students, and, graduating there, she and her friend had determined to go abroad to complete their education in Germany — the country then the ideal and goal of all studious Americans. The struggle to obtain this freedom for herself and for her friend had shaken Baltimore like an earthquake — a determination to devote themselves to lives of illrepute could hardly have created a greater scandal; but at last, after threats of suicide, hunger strikes, and other forms of awful defiance, they had achieved their purpose: they had gone, they were actually students at a German university. This was a turning toward Europe of a more serious kind than that of my grandfather, or than my father's brief participations in the religious circles abroad. The world of European learning, European scholarship, and German universities was what my intrepid cousin aimed at, and into which, to the unspeakable horror of Baltimore, she and her friend disappeared. In the great family conflict which had preceded this departure, my mother, who had always bitterly regretted that no opportunity for real education had been available for women in her youth, took passionately the side of her ambitious niece. Indeed, to the astonishment of everyone, her strict and disapproving mother, Friend Mary Whitall, the devotee of the correct Friend Gurney, expressed her approval of this wild project of her grandchild, and, when other supplies were all stopped, gave her the money for the voyage, calmly remarking, "I should have liked myself to have gone abroad to study."

Thus was diffused among us a dim apprehension of a world of study and scholarly ambitions centred in Germany, but with offshoots in England, and even possibly in America at Harvard, but remote, incredibly far away from our dull provincial Quaker community — indeed almost unheard of until this window in Baltimore had been so dramatically, so tempestuously, opened. I was destined later on to be decisively involved in the after-effects of this upheaval, but during my first two years at Haverford, of this I had no notion, set apart as I was to be a willing victim to the great Moloch and fiery furnace of our family business.

This was the point at which I had arrived when, in 1882, returning home again for the Easter holidays, I was told important news by my sister Mary, when she too arrived for her holidays from Smith College (for the ban on the college education of girls was now removed). There was a poet, she informed me and the rest of our family, a great American poet and prophet, — though most Americans were not at all aware of his greatness, — now living in poverty and neglect among us in America, living actually not far from our neighborhood, and it was her purpose, she informed us, to go without delay and offer him a due tribute of praise and admiration. How had she heard of this poet? her perturbed relatives inquired. A lady lecturer, she replied, had come from Boston to Smith College, and had praised his works, which she had herself immediately ordered from Boston, and which had revealed to her a message of tremendous import, and the purpose of her intended visit was to discuss this message. Consternation fell upon us all, and my father at once forbade it. He vaguely knew the name of the poet, which was by no means a name of good repute in Philadelphia; the district in which he lived was a district not visited by people who respected their own position; no daughter of his, he peremptorily declared, should, while she lived under his roof, be allowed to take so unseemly a step.

My father's refusal to permit this indecorum, though impressive as the poor man could make it, had no effect whatsoever upon my sister. She thought of going, she said, on the following Thursday; and my father, being in his heart well aware of the powerlessness of

American parents in their dealings with their daughters, and convinced, as he was, that if my sister meant to go on Thursday, on Thursday she would go, wisely, if unheroically, decided that the best thing under the circumstances was for him to accompany her, and thus lend an air of propriety to the visit. I was invited to join the party, and so on Thursday afternoon, off we started from our home in Germantown, behind my father's fine pair of horses. We flashed along through Fairmount Park, we drove across Philadelphia, we embarked in the ferry and crossed the Delaware, and dashed up before the little two-story wooden house in Camden to which we had been directed. An elderly woman who answered the doorbell ushered us into a little parlor and shouted upstairs, "Walt, here's some carriage folk come to see you." We heard a stirring above us as of a slow and unwieldy person, and soon through the open door we saw two large feet in carpet slippers slowly descending the stairs, and then the bulky form of the old man appeared before

[94]

Walt Whitman

us. Walt Whitman greeted us with friendly simplicity; he had no notion who we were, and we had no introduction to him, but the unannounced appearance of these "carriage folk" from across the river — this portly and opulent-looking gentleman with his tall son and beautiful tall daughter — did not seem to surprise him in the least. My sister informed him that our name was Smith, that she had read his *Leaves of Grass*, and had come to express her immense admiration for that volume, and this explanation was received with great complacency; we were all invited to follow him upstairs to his den, where we sat down on what chairs could be hastily provided, and were soon engaged in lively talk.

My father, who at first held himself aloof in the most disapproving manner, soon, to the surprise of my sister and myself, began to join in this friendly conversation, and we were still more surprised, when we got up to take our departure, to hear our impulsive parent invite the object of his grave disapprobation

[95]

to drive back with us to Germantown and spend the night. The afternoon was, he urged, a fine one, the drive across the Park would be pleasant, and it would be a pity to bring to a premature end so agreeable a confabulation. "No, Mr. Smith, I think I won't come," the poet answered; but when he had hobbled to the window and seen, waiting in the street outside, my father's equipage, he said that he thought he might as well come after all, and, hastily putting a nightshirt and a few other objects in a little bag, he hobbled downstairs and we all drove off together. It was, as my father had said, a pleasant afternoon; we crossed again the ferry, we drove through Philadelphia and through the Park to our home in Germantown, where Walt Whitman remained with us for a month, and whither he would often afterwards return. He became indeed a familiar and friendly inmate of the house, whose genial presence, even when we did not see him, could hardly pass unnoticed, for he had the habit of singing "Old Jim Crow" when not occupied in conversation, and his loud and cheerful voice could be heard echoing every morning from the bathroom or the water closet. His arrivals were always unannounced; he would appear when he liked, stay as long as he liked; and then one morning we would find at breakfast a penciled note to say that he had departed early, having had for the present enough of our society.

The reputation which the author of the *Leaves of Grass* had acquired by that daring and not decent publication was a dubious one in America at that time; this reputation had reached our Quaker suburb, and our neighbors and relations avoided our house, and forbade their children to visit it, when it was known that Walt Whitman was staying with us. There was, indeed, a grave charge which could have been brought against him, and which would have greatly shocked us all, if we had known (as we fortunately did not) anything about it. There can be no doubt, I fear, that from his boyhood Walt Whitman had associated with Hicksite Quakers, that his father and mother had been followers of this prophet, and that he himself had in his youth heard him preach. Indeed, in his old age he wrote a eulogy of this aged Quaker in which he described the long life of piety and benevolence of the saintly old man, and quoted without the least disapproval his doctrine that true religion consisted, not in sermons and ceremonials, but in spirituality, purity, and the love of God and man.

This eulogy of Elias Hicks was written perhaps by the naughty old poet while he was staying under our roof. But, as I say, one's sense of wrong grows weaker with the years, and the other day I read Walt Whitman's account of Elias Hicks with no overwhelming moral condemnation. Indeed it was difficult at any time for anyone to retain a prejudice against Walt Whitman for long. His manners were grand and primeval, like those of the old patriarchs and bards in a picture of Blake's; he treated all people with the same politeness, and only on one occasion did we notice in him any sense of times and occasions and the demands of social etiquette. He had arrived on a visit in a knitted vest, and, when told that a number of people were coming that evening to dinner, the thought occurred to him that probably he ought to put on a coat for the occasion, and after some meditation he appeared at dinner time a consummate man of the world in his overcoat, thus sacrificing his comfort, for the night was hot, to the demands of the occasion.

Almost every afternoon my father would take Walt Whitman driving in the Park; it was an unfailing interest to them to drive as close as they could behind buggies in which pairs of lovers were seated, and observe the degree of slope towards each other, or "buggy-angle," as they called it, of these couples; and if ever they saw this angle of approximation narrowed to an embrace, my father and Walt Whitman, who had ever honored that joy-giving power of nature symbolized under the name of Venus, would return home with happy hearts.

My acquaintanceship with this great and

famous poet, — for Walt Whitman had already become famous in England, and his glory had flashed back across the Atlantic to Boston, and thence, as I have described, to where we sat in Germantown in darkness, — the familiar presence of this poet in our house, must have had an influence upon me which was more powerful than anything that I was aware of at the time. He was, as John Burroughs has well described him, "large and picturesque of figure, slow of movement, tolerant, receptive, democratic and full of charity and good will towards all. His life was a poet's life from first to last — free, unworldly, unhurried, unconventional, unselfish, and was contentedly and joyously lived." He was already old and half-paralyzed when we made his acquaintance, but of the disabilities of age he never spoke, although their shadows are not absent from his poems of this period. In one of these, for instance, "Queries to My Seventieth Year," which was written just when we came to know him, he thus addresses the oncoming year: —

Approaching, nearing curious,
Thou dim, uncertain spectre — bringest thou life or
 death ?
Strength, weakness, blindness, more paralysis and
 heavier ?
Or placid skies and sun ? Wilt stir the waters yet ?
Or haply cut me short for good ? Or leave me here
 as now,
Dull, parrot-like and old, with crack'd voice harp-
 ing, screeching ?

It was, however, the calm serenity of age,
its placid skies and sun, which diffused about
him that atmosphere of peace and leisure
which made his companionship so genial, and
our endless conversations with him so great a
pleasure. He was fond of talking with young
people, and would listen with the utmost good
nature to our crude notions; and when he was
not with us, my sisters and I would often visit
him in Camden, where on summer days we
would find him seated at his window, fanning
himself with a large palm-leaf fan, and gazing
out on the lazy sunshine that filled his little
street. Not infrequently during our visits he
would recognize some workingman of his ac-

quaintance as he passed, and call out, "Come up, Bill, and meet some friends of mine," and the workingman would come in, or the passing postman, or the driver of an express wagon, and we would all share an improvised meal together.

The floor of the room upstairs in which he lived was covered to the depth of a foot or so with a sea of papers, and now and then he would stir this pool with his stick and fish up a letter from an English admirer — Tennyson perhaps, or Symonds, or Edward Dowden — or some newspaper article about "the Good Grey Poet." Walt Whitman, who had been himself so long a newspaper writer, was curiously fond of newspaper publicity; his floor was strewn with press cuttings in which his name was mentioned, and he would even, I believe, now and then, write anonymous articles about himself for insertion in the local papers. Otherwise he was quite free from literary vanity, and never spoke of his writings unless we questioned him. Then, however, he would answer with great simplicity and frankness.

Walt Whitman

My sister Mary (whom he called his "bright, particular star") recalls how once, when she was on the Camden ferry, she saw an Englishman also on the boat. He must, she rightly concluded, be on a pilgrimage like herself to visit Walt Whitman, for how otherwise account for the presence of that Englishman? She, therefore, accosted the correct and dapper figure, who confessed, with some surprise, that this was in fact his purpose. My sister offered to show him the way to Walt Whitman's house, and they proceeded thither, to find, however, that the door was locked and they could get no answer to their knockings. "I'm sure he's upstairs," my sister said; "he always is, so the best thing is for me to boost you up to the window, which you can open, and then come down and let me in." Edmund Gosse (for the Englishman was Edmund Gosse) seemed considerably surprised, my sister says, by the unconventionality of this proposal, but as he had come a long way to visit Walt Whitman, and did not wish to be baffled in his object, he finally

[103]

allowed my sister to boost him up; and then he descended to open the front door to her, and they found Walt Whitman as usual in his study, and their visit was a satisfactory one in every way. It is only fair, however, to add that when, thirty or forty years after, I arranged for Mrs. Berenson and Sir Edmund Gosse to meet at luncheon, the latter, though admitting that he had met my sister at Walt Whitman's, angrily denied the boosting and his informal entrance. Knowing both Gosse and my sister to be endowed with more picturesque than accurate memories, I have never been able to decide which of them was telling the truth.

I remember once speaking to Walt Whitman about his poem, "With husky-haughty lips, O sea!" which had just been published, and he told me, sitting one summer evening on our porch in Germantown, of the way he had come to write it; how always, from the days of his boyhood on the Long Island coasts, he had tried and tried again to seize the meaning which the voice of the ocean was

always whispering in his ears; how often by
day, and more often by night, he had sat or
lain amid the sandhills on its margin, listening
in a kind of torment of attention to that great
voice — some voice — in what words could
he best describe it?

. . . some voice, in huge monotonous rage, of
  freedom-lover pent,
Some vast heart, like a planet's, chain'd and chaf-
  ing in those breakers.

This notion of receptivity to experience, and
of a complete surrender to it, combined with
a patient effort to grasp its deepest meaning
and to embody that meaning in significant
words — this account of the old man's poetic
method, as he told it one summer evening,
was deeply impressive to his boyish listener,
although that listener had then no thought
of attempting to coin his own experience into
enduring metal. To melt material sand into
salable glass bottles — this, he believed, was
to be his destiny; and the idea that all such
massy unmetaphorical gold might be gladly
bartered — as Walt Whitman would gladly

have bartered it — for the ability to embody in words some one of Nature's aspects, — the sea's voice, for instance, or the breath of its salt fragrance, or even, as he himself had said, "the undulation of one wave," — the idea of so mad a preference would have seemed to his youthful listener at that date fantastic indeed.

Thus I listened to the impressive talk of the old poet, and though I had no notion of following his example, the effect upon me of his poems, as I read and reread that strange volume, the *Leaves of Grass* — how can I adequately describe it? There are books which come to us like revelations, which, as Emerson says, "take rank in our lives with parents and lovers and passionate experiences," and to come on such a book to which one can yield oneself in absolute surrender — there is no intellectual enjoyment, I believe, no joy of the mind greater in youth than this. Books of this kind should be contemporary books, written by the living for the living; and should pre-

sent us with a picture of life as we ourselves
know it and feel it. And they should above all
reveal us to ourselves, should hold up a looking glass before our eyes in which we see our
own faces. Much that was suppressed in the
young people of my generation found a frank
avowal in the *Leaves of Grass;* feelings and
affections for each other, which we had been
ashamed of, thoughts which we had hidden
as unutterable, we found printed in its pages,
discovering that they were not, as we had
believed, the thoughts and feelings of young,
guilty, half-crazy goblins, but portions of the
Kingdom of Truth and the sane experience of
mankind. It was above all Walt Whitman's
rejoicing in his flesh and blood, — "there is
so much of me," he sang, "and all so lus-
cious," — his delight in his own body and the
bodies of his friends, which seemed a revelation and gave the *Leaves of Grass* so strong a
hold upon a generation born of puritans who
had ignored, or treated as shameful, those
habitations of the spirit. Then, too, Walt
Whitman's affection for his fellow human

beings, — for he was one of those rare spirits who really love the human race, — his feeling that all men and women, of whatever race or class and in whatever state of degradation, were all of them not worthless and of no account, but lovable and mysterious and divine — this seemed to fill for us the many-peopled world with innumerable creatures, all dear and infinitely precious. These were the streams of life which flowed from that fountain; and catching also from its pages the fervor of his exultant pride in Democracy, in America and the age we lived in, and moved also by the splendid passages here and there of great poetry, it is no wonder that we came to regard as a sacred book the vast printed chaos of the *Leaves of Grass*. It gave us ears, it gave us eyes, it revealed to us the miracle of our own existence, and for me, at least, with my meagre ideals of borrowed culture, it seemed to open a great shining window in my narrow house of life.

4

Harvard

AT THIS TIME I was still an under-graduate at Haverford; but in 1884, when I was nineteen years old, I went to Harvard from that small Quaker college. In this translation, I was still following in the footsteps of my aspiring elder sister, who had awakened my taste for literature, who had brought Walt Whitman to our house, and who had now decided to leave Smith College for the superior feminine institution which had recently been founded in the shade of America's oldest and most famous university. My sister's upward flights, though never unaccompanied by swarms of wooers, were inspired by a genuine ardor for intellectual things, and she was bent on applying her excellent young mind to the study of philosophy.

This philosophic interest had been, I will not say awakened, but certainly enhanced by an incident which happened in the summer of 1883, and which was destined to have a considerable influence on her life, and on that of all our family, including my own. In the summer of this year the British Association met in Canada, and many of its members toured the United States, and came in due course to Philadelphia, whose citizens were requested to open their houses for the entertainment of these visitors from abroad. Five of them were allotted by the local committee to us, and came to stay at our house in Germantown, and of these five, three fell at once in love with my sister.

One of them was a professor of some distinction at an Irish university, and one a don at Christ Church. The third was a young London barrister of Irish origin, a Balliol graduate and favorite pupil of Benjamin Jowett's. Though a fervent Roman Catholic, he had somehow reconciled his beliefs with the Hegelianism then current at Oxford. Much would

[110]

he talk of Balliol College and of its revered Master, Benjamin Jowett, who had prophesied for him a shining future; of T. H. Green, and Arnold Toynbee and Toynbee Hall and its new philanthropy; of English Liberalism and its great leader Gladstone; and of the great radical, Joe Chamberlain, under whose banner it was his hope and purpose to march to triumph for the great causes he had espoused. This triumph was, we were given to understand, to be accompanied by fame and beneficent power for himself. These great names, the names of T. H. Green, and Jowett, of Arnold Toynbee and Gladstone and Joe Chamberlain, awake somewhat ironic echoes as I now repeat them; but then, at least in our remote Philadelphia environment, they sounded like the names of heroes shouted from afar.

It is no wonder, therefore, that to this music my aspiring sister would seriously incline her ears — ears which afterwards she came to think of as having been at that time somewhat gullible organs of audition. The middle-aged professor, the middle-aged don from Christ Church, had no spells like these to weave; they soon faded away across the Atlantic; but the aspiring barrister's suggestion, which he urged with passionate eloquence upon my sister, that she should become his partner and fellow fighter in this great contemporary effort to bring the Kingdom of Heaven down to earth, in England — this shining prospect began more and more to engage her grave attention. What impressed her most, and struck her as indeed momentous and imposing, was the broad and deep foundations upon which this proposed New Jerusalem was to be founded, this splendid castle of his evocation, on whose high towers she was thus invited to build with him their eagle's nest.

Nothing less fundamental could have satisfied her. Modern philosophy and modern science had shaken, she felt, her belief in the old evangelical explanation of the universe; but now to be assured, to be half-convinced by this accomplished dialectician, that on the very philosophy, the very science, which had daunted her, they could, by sounding to the darkest abysses, build up together the great edifice of Faith, and thus restore again those great watchwords, "God," "Duty," and "Immortality," which were, he added, requisite for her salvation and the salvation of the human race; that they would moreover prove all this — O marvelous! — to be eternally riveted on the firm basis of the ancient and Catholic universal Church — this was indeed a high-flying courtship and a splendid wooing, and she was profoundly impressed (how could it be otherwise?) by the prospect.

To soar, however, into so exalted a region it would be necessary, she felt, for her to expand her intellectual wings; she must, in fact, study philosophy with more attention; and for that study Harvard, with its famous philosophers, Royce and William James and Professor Palmer, was obviously the place. So from Smith College my sister transferred herself to Cambridge, and, as I have said, I followed in her train. This migration was the more easily effected owing to William James's friendship with my parents. He was an admirer of my mother's religious writings; he had enlisted my father's assistance in the formation of an American Society for Psychical Research, and had more than once stayed with us in Germantown when he came to Philadelphia in connection with this work. It was, I think, by his arrangement that lodgings were found for my sister and myself in the comfortable home of two elderly Cambridge maiden ladies; and a new chapter in our lives began.

Though my sister and I lodged together, we led our lives in complete disassociation. She began at once her philosophic studies; and at once, for it was her fate, the only professor who was willing to instruct her joined himself in a headlong fashion to the band of her wooers, and began to endeavor, by displaying another metaphysic, to replace in her thoughts, and ultimately at the matrimonial altar, the London barrister with whom, as he knew, she was engaged at that time in a correspondence which much occupied her mind. While this philosophic and yet passionate drama (in which I did not take the slightest interest) was proceeding, was in fact, I may say, raging, — and the word is not too strong, for the professor's eager courtship of a young woman who attended his lectures did more honor to his temperament than credit to the chair he occupied, — while all this was going on, I became more and more absorbed in the pleasant social life of Harvard.

My father had given me a generous allowance. I had already a few acquaintances who belonged to what was considered a good set among the undergraduates, and was elected a member of several of those societies and fraternities which play, or played, so important a part in Harvard life. I have now forgotten the names of these foolish associations, but my pleasure at my election to them I can still recall. It was in the essence a snobbish pleasure; why should I boggle at the word? Indeed the atmosphere of Harvard was at that time — whether it has changed since then, I do not know — richly colored by the sense of social differences. The prestige possessed by members of the most exclusive clubs, the delight of being seen in their company, and the hope of being admitted into their select circles — these were the animating motives of life at Harvard as I knew it; and the democratic principles I had learned from Walt Whitman were of little avail against this atmosphere of social aspiration. That there was an intellectual set at Harvard of much greater interest than the foolish world in which I was, after all, little more than an outsider; that there were young men of intelligence and high promise among my contemporaries, I had not the slightest notion. I was indeed hardly worthy at that time of the notice of intellectuals like Santayana and Berenson, who were at Harvard with me, though I did not know them, and with whom I became acquainted only in after years.

I actually sat beside my present brother-in-law, Berenson, at a course of William James's lectures, but no communication passed between us, and it was not till long afterwards, when he had married my elder sister, that we began that series of confabulations to which I owe so much. For my parents' sake William James did, however, befriend their callow offspring, and I was often invited to his hospitable house. I need not try to describe the charm of the most charming man I ever met; Ralph Perry has performed that task in his admirable biography, but I may perhaps add a touch to his account of that free and spontaneous spirit by repeating an anecdote he related to me one night, telling me that I might repeat it anywhere but in Cambridge.

He had gone, he told me, by tram that afternoon to Boston; and as he sat and meditated in the Cambridge horsecar two strains of thought had occupied his mind. One of these was the notion, which Mrs. James had recently derived from the perusal of Kipling's writings, that our civil order, that all the graces and amenities of our social life, had for their ultimate sanction nothing but force, however much we might disguise it — the naked fist, in fact, the blow of the sword, the crack of the pistol, or the smoke and roar of guns. Superimposed upon this meditation began to recur, with greater and greater persistence, the memory of certain remarks of his brother Henry, who, on a recent visit to America, had indignantly protested against the outrageous pertness of the American child and the meek pusillanimity with which the older generation suffered the behavior of their children without protest.

It was not long, William James said, before he became aware of what had aroused this second line of thought; it was the droning sound which filled the horsecar — the voice, in fact, of an American child, who was squeaking over and over again an endless, shrill, monotonous singsong. Growing more and more irritated by this squeaking, William James resolved that he at least would not suffer it without protest; so, addressing the mother of the vocal infant, he said politely, "I think, madam, you can hardly be aware that your child's song is a cause of annoyance to the rest of us in this car." The lady thus addressed paid no attention; but a gallant American, who heard it, turned on him and said with great indignation, "How dare you, sir, address a lady in this ungentlemanly fashion!" At this insult William James, recalling the doctrine of naked force which his wife had impressed upon him, replied with manly promptness, "Sir, if you repeat that remark, I shall slap your face." The remark, to his consternation, was repeated, and the professor was compelled to make good his word. The slap was conscientiously administered; the occupants of the horsecar arose in indignation, pressing their cards upon the victim of the assault, and protesting their willingness to be witnesses at any legal proceedings which might ensue. Then they all sat down; and as the car clattered along through the dust towards Boston, with the child still shrilly singing, the grave burden of the public disapproval which William James had encountered became almost more, he said, than he could bear.

He looked from hostile face to hostile face, longing for some sign of sympathy and comprehension, and fixed at last all his hopes on a lady who had taken no part in the uproar, and whose appearance suggested foreign travel perhaps, or at any rate a wider point of view. He felt that she at least understood the motive of his action; and so great was his longing for sympathy that when at last the car reached Boston and they all got out he committed the error of trying to make sure of her approbation. "You, madam," he said, addressing her, "you, I feel sure, will understand . . ." Thereupon the lady drew back from him and exclaimed, "You brute!"

I may add here another anecdote of William James, for when I name that enchanting person it is difficult to dismiss him with no further mention. Some years later, when our family was at last established abroad, he came to stay with us in Sussex, and declared his desire to spend a summer in England and experience the joys of English country life. My father thereupon obtained a list of country houses to be let in our neighborhood, and orders to view them, and drove William James to see one after the other. This inspection he carried on with the utmost care, examining each house from attic to cellar, allotting the various rooms to be occupied by the various members of his family. When this process was over, and the gardens and even the stables had been examined, and he returned to our house to dinner, he genially remarked, "I can't tell you how grateful I am for all the trouble you have taken; I have had my summer in England, and now we go abroad."

While we were at Harvard, Edmund Gosse came to Boston to deliver the Lowell Lectures; my sister and many of the Harvard intellectuals went religiously to listen to the utterance of this English writer, whose name was familiar to us all. Of these lectures I have forgotten everything except one pregnant sentence, in which the name of Botticelli first echoed in our ears. "Botticelli," the lecturer said, in that cultivated "English accent" which was music to us, "Botticelli," — and with what unction he slowly reiterated those syllables! — "Botticelli, that name which is an open sesame to the most select, the most distinguished, the most exclusive circles of European culture." The effect of these words upon us was magical. What longings it aroused in us, what delicious provincial aspirations for a world fairer than the world we lived in — for exquisite, remote, European things! It was the song the Syrens sang, it was the voice of the Muses that Thamyris heard among the Theban mountains, it was almost the voice that summoned Saint Paul to a higher life as he journeyed to Damascus. Would Fate, we deliciously wondered, ever vouchsafe to us to enunciate those syllables of sweet magic and thus win admission to those far-away bright circles of European culture, circles as heavenly in our provincial eyes as those circling rings of angels seen in great Italian pictures? Among that audience, although my sister and I did not know him at the time, was the future art critic, Bernard

[122]

Berenson, who, he has told us since, went at once and bought himself a reproduction of Botticelli's "Primavera."

Life is an ironic thing, and when years afterwards I recalled to Sir Edmund Gosse the words which he had pronounced long ago in Boston, he told me that his principal association with the name of Botticelli at that time was connected with the family cat, Beneder, which was then by its mewings causing considerable annoyance in his household. There had been a joke in *Punch* about an æsthete who, when shown a picture attributed to Botticelli, had denied its authenticity on the ground that he was always dumb in the presence of a work of that master. So the Gosses had purchased a photograph of an unquestioned picture by Botticelli, and pinned it up by the basket of Beneder, in the hope, which proved a vain one, of silencing its voice.

I have spoken of the effect upon me of Walt Whitman's poems; I fell at Harvard (for my time there was not utterly wasted) under the influence of another living writer, Matthew Arnold. When I now think of Matthew Arnold, it makes me rather sad. The exquisite poet who so soon abandoned poetry; the supreme critic whose best criticism is so scanty; the great writer who wasted the energy of his best years in dull official routine; the advocate of Hellenism and sweet reasonableness who soon gave himself up to angry recrimination, and who, whether owing to exasperation with his contemporaries or to some arrogant streak in his own nature, more and more abandoned that serene aloofness from contemporary conflicts which had been his ideal, and adopted a pose of aggressive, self-satisfied contempt, and a harsh browbeating style full of derisive catchwords.

When I read again the best writings of Matthew Arnold I find in them the expression of the most truly enlightened spirit among the great Victorians, the most humane, the most European and least provincial of all English authors, whose outlook is still our outlook, who still speaks to us with contemporary

accents. But fifty years ago it was that more
controversial Matthew Arnold who aroused
my young enthusiasm. His aggressive warfare with the Philistines delighted me; I rejoiced in his ridicule of the evangelical religion
and dissent in which I had been nourished,
and what delighted me most of all was his
attribution of an arrogant superiority, an
exclusive kind of distinction to that culture,
that sweetness and light, which now for the
flimsiest reasons I believed that I had attained. But it was not only the attainment of
culture for oneself, but the diffusion of it,
which Matthew Arnold preached, and this
part of his doctrine was most of all an inspiration to me.

I belonged by family traditions to the philanthropic world; from the American atmosphere and from the conversations and the
writings of Walt Whitman I had absorbed
democratic principles which floated vaguely
— as such principles can easily float without
conflict — side by side with my more exclusive proclivities, and above all with an ideal

of cultural uplift, as it would now be called. I found that I could gild with a finer gold than that of dollars my future commercial prospects. I imagined myself as returning, when I entered the family business, to my birthplace amid its furnaces in New Jersey, to diffuse among those raw and illiberal workmen a love of beauty, a passion for things of the mind and a desire to learn the best that is known and thought in the world. I saw myself a picturesque, a somewhat pathetic figure (for the children of light are lonely in this world and are almost always persecuted by it), awakening in these unenlightened employees of my family their more delicate and spiritual perceptions, and by a most happy combination of circumstances drawing all the while a large income from my activities among them.

Thus Matthew Arnold's oft-repeated watchwords of "sweetness and light" and "warfare against the Philistines" were words of enchantment in my ears; and another doctrine of his, that of "many-sided culture," served usefully also to justify and ennoble the extremely many-sided, not to say miscellaneous studies — if they may be called studies — which engaged a small part of my attention during my sojourn at Harvard.

Following the example and enjoying the companionship of my gay and unstudious companions, I had fallen in with the strange custom which then prevailed at that university (things are changed now for the better, I believe) of attending miscellaneous and perfectly unrelated lecture courses — courses recommended more for what was called their "softness" than for any other reason; going to lectures, for instance, at the same time on Dante and Meteorology, on Homer and on the practice of philanthropy, and other unconnected subjects. If this was a strange method of acquiring the many-sided culture Matthew Arnold recommended, its strangeness never occurred to me, nor was it ever suggested by any of my instructors.

I perceive that I got almost nothing of intellectual value from Harvard University. It was my fault, no doubt; if I had been a real student, I should have found genuine instruction. But, for all my assumption of superiority, the crudeness of my mind at the age of twenty wakens amazement in me. Though I read the works of Matthew Arnold, I gave equal or perhaps more serious attention to the literature of Theosophy, and was inclined to believe that the key to the problem of existence was to be found, if I could only grasp it, in a little book of Rosicrucian doctrine over which I used to pore for hours. My sister, with her superior philosophic light, scorned my Rosicrucian speculations, but she herself visited at this time, with the intention of studying her doctrine, the famous female prophet, Mrs. Mary Baker Eddy; nor was she much better able than I to discriminate between all the various names — Botticelli and Benjamin Jowett and Mrs. Eddy and Matthew Arnold and Gladstone and William James and the Rosy Cross — which sounded in our ears.

I detect in myself a tendency to sentimentalize over these early years of my existence.

Harvard

It is not that I wish to recall my youth. It is rather that I feel a kind of impatient pity for that half-baked young fool of an American boy about whom I have been writing. No, I have no regrets for youth. Gladly would I go on living at my present age, and with my present interests, for uncounted years. To become young again would seem to me an appalling prospect. Youth is a kind of delirium, which can only be cured, if it is ever cured at all, by years of painful treatment.

The debt of our civilization to the ancient Greeks is of course beyond all calculation, but in one respect we have no cause to thank them. Their adoration of the youthful human form, in contrast to the Eastern idealization of venerable age, has put a kind of blight on human life; our progress, as we grow older, in wisdom and humanity is thought of in terms of the physical decay which accompanies that luminous advance. We feel ashamed, instead of feeling proud like the Chinese, of our accumulating years; we are always trying in vain to seem younger than we really are; and in our Western world it is by no means a compliment, as it is in the wise East, to attribute to others a greater age than their appearance might suggest. When I think of that brother and sister fifty years ago at Harvard, — endowed, it may be, with the grace of youth, but full otherwise of ignorance and folly, — I cannot but prize more highly our present state. Our bones are ripening, it is true, for their ultimate repose, but how small a price, after all, is that to pay for the knowledge we have acquired of the world and men, for the splendid panorama of literature and the arts which years of travel and study have unrolled before us, and above all for those adequate conceptions in whose possession, according to Spinoza's wisdom, true felicity consists.

5

Business and Release

IN THIS state of ignorance and folly
my sister and I finished our year at
Harvard, and joined the rest of our
family, my father and my mother and my
younger sister, in another jaunt abroad. My
elder sister was now about to end her high
prenuptial flight; the image of the Harvard
professor had been dimmed by that of the
English barrister, with his grandiose scheme
of bringing heaven to earth under the leader-
ship of Gladstone and Joe Chamberlain, and
beneath a banner inscribed with the great
watchwords of Hegelian logic, and yet bearing the authentic papal seal. She was to be
married in Oxford to this son of Balliol, and
the unprecedented glory was to be hers of a
wedding breakfast in that college hall, over
which the great Benjamin Jowett himself was

to preside. I was to be present at this cere-
mony, and then to be allowed a year of grace
in Europe, to finish my education by spending the winter at a German university, and
thus acquire some tincture of that German
learning which was considered by Americans
in the eighties as the flower and crown of culture.

After this European jaunt (there was a
taste in my family, as I have said, for these
jaunts abroad), I was to return to that bottle
business in Philadelphia which I regarded as
my fate.

This programme was punctually carried
out: my sister was married in Oxford to
Benjamin Costelloe; there was a big wedding
breakfast in the Hall at Balliol; the Master
presided and made a speech, and to these fes-
tivities my parents invited their evangelical
and especially their Quaker friends, who most
of them had condoned, if they had not forgotten, the scandal of my father's adventures
with his feminine disciples. At this gathering
I became aware of one curious phenomenon

[132]

which at the time I failed to understand. The
English Quakers who were our guests seemed
unwilling to mix together, and they separated
into little clans, and it was only later that I
came to realize that these "Friends," as they
were called, were divided among themselves
by not very friendly distinctions, each group
keeping aloof from the class which in wealth
or social position it considered inferior to itself. The same hierarchical divisions exist, I
have since discovered, among the English
Jews — another race, like the Quakers, who
live separated from the world, and yet in whom
the worldly spirit of caste is especially acute.

I went in the following autumn to Berlin,
where I lodged with a German family, and
attended the lectures of some of the famous
professors in that university, and heard many
concerts and operas, for I had been caught
by the fashionable craze for Wagner, and was
an enthusiastic though ignorant admirer of
his music. Save for the German I learned, and
the German books I read, I drew no real

profit from my sojourn there, and only one encounter of that winter stands out in my memory with any great distinctness. In my Wagner enthusiasm I used to go sometimes to Dresden, where the great operas were performed with especial éclat, and on one of these week-end visits I happened to find in my hotel a Russian family whose acquaintance I had previously made in traveling. I joined them in the hotel dining room, and they informed me with much amusement, for they were keen observers of characters and types, that there was staying in the hotel a genuine English "dog," as they called him — a "snob," a "sportsman" of the true authentic breed. The door soon opened; "There he is!" they cried, as a tall figure in a suit of large checks, and with a broad face and black whiskers, marched in with the jaunty air of an English schoolmaster who, in traveling abroad, assumes what he considers a man-of-the-world deportment.

My amazement (indeed horror is not too strong a word for my feelings) can be imagined when this whiskered face began to display the features of my revered poet and prophet — features which I knew well from photographs. So this was the author of the *Strayed Reveller* and *Thyrsis* and many poems I knew by heart — the exquisite apostle of that doctrine of sweetness and light which I had made my own! Matthew Arnold (for it really was Matthew Arnold) approached the table at which we sat, and, slapping down a pair of big tan gloves before those Russian ladies, began to entertain them with an account of the very favorable reception he had received at the Saxon Court from certain dear princesses who were his especial friends. I looked at this large, cheerful figure, I listened to his boastful conversation, with dismay. What I had expected Matthew Arnold to be like, what Apollonian aspect I had imagined for his face, and what divine discourse I had hoped to hear from his lips I hardly knew, but this was certainly not what I should have looked for, and my disillusion (I was only twenty) was almost overwhelming.

Unforgotten Years

But at this time men of letters like Matthew Arnold, like Browning, and like the younger Henry James, had formed the habit of wearing masks, which saved them no doubt from much impertinence and tiresome gush about their writings; and as the world, with its standards of good form and deportment, was then taken more seriously than anyone takes it now, the masks they assumed were worldly ones.

During my stay at Dresden I often heard Matthew Arnold impress the table d'hôte with his tales of the Saxon Court. "Not here, O Apollo, are haunts meet for thee," I murmured to myself; but I never dared to speak to him of literature, or of my passionate love for his writings. He treated me, however, with jolly kindness, and invited me to come and stay with him in England; but either because he died not long after, or because I was afraid of further disillusion, I never saw him again. Of course he did not want to talk of literature with the rather insufferable young prig he had met by chance in a Dresden hotel, and I dare say the impression of him that remains in my memory is a false one. But he certainly was a very different kind of poet from Walt Whitman.

I specially remember how shocked I was when, after sitting in ecstatic reverence at a splendid performance of the *Valkyrie*, I ventured to ask him, as we walked back together to the hotel, what impression the music had made upon him. "Oh, I had to go," he said in his offhand manner, "but I only went because my wife and daughters would have scoffed at me if I had n't. But if you ask me what I thought of it — well, it seemed to me — like — what shall I say? — it seemed to me the sort of thing that I should have composed myself if I happened to try my hand at composing music." "Oh, Matthew Arnold," I murmured to myself, "is this the way you strive for a many-sided perfection; is it thus that you listen with particular heed to those voices of foreign culture which are especially likely to escape us in our provincial Anglo-Saxon darkness?"

[137]

In the autumn of 1886, I returned with my mother and father and younger sister to America, leaving my elder sister settled in London to engage with her barrister husband in that reminting, by means of Hegelian philosophy, of the three great religious watchwords, "God," "Duty," and "Immortality," under whose auspices, and that of the Catholic Church, Jerusalem was to be planted in England. These processes of reminting and Jerusalem-building seemed somehow to our uninitiated eyes to have been for the moment postponed to the exigencies of our new relative's career at the bar and in politics.

The Master of his College, Benjamin Jowett, the inspirer and guide of generations of able and ambitious young Balliol men, had formed the useful habit of pronouncing before each of his favorites as they departed some pregnant word or sentence suited to their character and prospects — a kind of apophthegm or maxim to be their watchword in their careers; and at his parting with my brother-in-law he had sententiously remarked,

Business and Release

"It is most important in this world, Costelloe, to be pushing; but," he added, after a pregnant pause, "it is fatal to seem so." The earlier part of this wise saying my new brother-in-law seemed to have appropriated to himself with enthusiasm, but somewhat, it was said by those who did not like him, to the neglect of the hint implied in the second clause. However that might be, the newly married couple were almost lost to us in a rush of political and social engagements, into which my sister seemed to enter with enthusiasm and the highest hopes, while we returned from our jaunt across the Atlantic, and I prepared with some reluctance to begin my business career.

I say "with some reluctance," for though I did not doubt the validity of the great principle on which I was acting, or question the golden nature of my prospects, my jaunt to Europe, my wanderings about the Continent, had given me a taste for life abroad which caused a certain repining; and above all I remembered having been present at a service in an Oxford chapel, and feeling, as one of the white-robed scholars read the evening lesson, a pang of regret that no such pleasant college life could ever be enjoyed by me. These, however, were but vague regrets; the thought would have seemed insane of abandoning the golden plum which hung ripe for my grasp upon the family tree. If my dream of being an apostle of enlightenment amid the family furnaces and diffusing culture among those glass blowers had, owing to my advance in age, and perhaps to my unhappy meeting with Matthew Arnold, grown somewhat dimmer, I had replaced it by the more practicable if less exalted ideal of retiring from business early — after, say, twenty years, when I had acquired a modest sufficiency of this world's goods which would allow me to live a life of cultured leisure. Not in Europe, however, but in some more cultivated American corner, for I was a good patriot, and my condemnation and contempt were great for those Americans who abandoned their country to lead idle and probably corrupt lives in foreign parts.

Business and Release

I have already mentioned my Baltimore cousin, Carey Thomas, who had gone to study abroad and had opened for us a window on the truer, more scholarly culture of European learning. Miss Thomas had now returned, and was busy in applying her ideals to the modeling of that new-founded Quaker college for women which has since become famous under the name of Bryn Mawr College. Miss Thomas had apparently not lost, amid this constructive work, her taste for smashing windows to let in new light; and, though extremely busy, she summoned me to an interview at Bryn Mawr. I did not know my cousin well; she was nine years older than myself, at an age when nine years makes a tremendous difference, and the half-legendary tales of her academic success had produced in me an immense awe and respect for her person and opinions. I approached this interview with some trepidation, which was, however, nothing compared to what it would have been had I known the awful words she had determined to pronounce.

"So thee is going into the family business?" she abruptly began.

"Why, certainly, of course," I replied. "How could I dream of anything else?"

"Well," said my cousin, "I'd rather shoot myself."

Was it possible that I had heard her rightly, or had my distinguished relative suddenly gone mad? "But Carey," I protested, "it's a most splendid chance — a chance in ten thousand, to take my father's place in a great expanding business."

"I'd rather shoot myself," the awful woman repeated, and this time I could not doubt the words I heard.

"But," I protested, "it may be a chance to make a fortune!"

"Why make a fortune?" was the answer.

"But Carey —" I protested.

"What's the good of money?" she interrupted. "Look at our cousins who have gone into the business; they've all become dull old men before their time. What good has their money done them? What on earth do they get out of it? Is thee really going to sacrifice thy life to become one of them?"

In my need to argue with this mad, misguided cousin, I fell back on my old ideal — which, though it had somewhat faded, I had not completely abandoned — of entering the family business to spread among those glass blowers the ideal of a many-sided culture. "Bosh!" was, if I remember rightly, my cousin's answer on this occasion, and to this energetic monosyllable I found I had no reply. My second ideal, of making a modest but sufficient income and retiring after, say, twenty years, seemed irrefutable, and was now put forward.

"But why waste those twenty years?" my cousin queried. "The best, the most important, the most pleasant years of life. Wait twenty years and it 'll be too late. Too late," she ominously repeated.

"But Carey," I almost bleated, "I have n't any money."

"Thee needs very little money," she answered. "I lived abroad on five hundred dol-

lars a year. Make thy father give thee that —
he can easily give thee more."

"And abandon my country?" I asked.
"Go abroad and give up America, with its
need for culture and cultivated people?"

"Bosh!" again answered my cousin.

"But what should I do abroad?" I queru-
lously inquired.

"Thee might take up writing," Miss Thomas suggested.

"But I have no talent, not the slightest
gleam of talent for writing," I protested.

"Then go and live at Monte Carlo and
enjoy thyself," was the advice of this eminent Quaker to her young Quaker cousin of
twenty-one; whereupon I was dismissed, and
went away indignant and amazed. What?
To give up and madly throw away the prospect of a fortune, and go and live abroad on a
pittance in some shabby pension; to desert
my country, and break the heart of my father,
who, as he had often reiterated, had only
been sustained in his toils and travails by the
thought that I, his only son, should succeed

[144]

him and reap the benefit of his sacrifices! All this seemed something dreadful, portentous, inexplicable — the result, perhaps, of a temporary aberration, or of some perversion my cousin had contracted abroad.

Putting aside, therefore, the memory of this interview, and trying to forget it, I cheerfully entered the temple of Mammon, and its iron gates clanged behind me. My parents had gone abroad again, and it had been conceded, since New York was more a centre of culture than Philadelphia, that I should be attached to the New York branch of the family business. I was to enter that office at the bottom, working like the humblest clerk, and being paid the most modest wage. So to New York I went, and engaged a couple of rooms high up in one of its apartment buildings. These rooms I adorned with photographs of the " Mona Lisa " and a few other famous pictures; I had my books, my Matthew Arnold, my Balzac, my Blake reproductions; and then my business life began.

I cannot honestly say that I was unhappy during my year in New York. Most human beings are born for harness and are melancholy when out of it too long. Like Wordsworth, they feel the weight of chance desires; the definite routine, the daily necessary task, eliminates the need for self-imposed activity, and they are freed from that irresolution, that temptation to postponement, that degrading sophistry of laziness which is the curse of those whose tasks are voluntary and can be performed at any time. My hours of work were long, but absolutely regular: I was at the warehouse at eight o'clock; I departed at six or seven, healthily fatigued, and ready to enjoy an evening of reading, music, or other pleasant relaxation. I was naturally industrious, and not, I think, devoid of business talent; my tasks, though uninteresting, were not difficult, and I enjoyed fulfilling them with efficiency.

If I had no favor owing to my family connections, I was aware of no jealousy on the part of my fellow clerks, and I suffered no kind of persecution from them. My modest wages, the dollar notes which I received every Saturday, were precious to me from the fact that I had honestly earned them. They seemed more valuable, more authentic, more like real money than any of the bestowed currency which had ever before got into my pocket. And I certainly tasted one joy during this year of business which I have never tasted since — the joy of Sunday, of that precious day of golden leisure, the memory of which, and the prospect of its sure recurrence, sweetened all the intervening days of work. Now all my days are Sundays; no one of them stands out among the others to bestow a special felicity, or shines with an illumination of its own. Thus I underwent my apprentice-ship, learning my task better and better, and apparently beginning, under the best auspices, a prosperous business career.

I have read somewhere of men who receive a wound which they hardly notice, and often carry on for a long time their ordinary activ-ities, quite unaware that they have been stricken in a vital part. That was really my condition, although I did n't know it, all that winter: a kind of ominous suppressed questioning, a mysterious unending argument, seemed to be going on in my unconscious self, and reverberations from it would rise every now and then into my thoughts. "It's ridiculous," I would catch myself asserting, "to say that money is no good — she knows absolutely nothing of the world." I began a determined process of trying to idealize money, to convince myself that I did want fine houses, opulence, and good food. Above all I tried to fix my mind on the satisfaction, so much enjoyed by my father, of dashing along with the gleam and rattle of harness behind a pair of fine horses. And yet to sacrifice one's life for this, to toil day after day, year after year, till youth was over? How was my gold grown dim, my fine gold tarnished!

I read and reread Henry James's stories of Americans abroad; pictures of my foreign travels would shine and fade in the background of my mind, and more persistently of all, perhaps, the memory of that afternoon at Oxford when I had seen a handsome white-robed youth read the lesson in his college chapel. I began to wonder if all the wealth the world could give would compensate for the deprivation of the pleasures which Europe offered; and little by little the longing for a life of cultivated leisure, or at least of vague æsthetic experience, grew upon me. But I was still the dupe of that cleverest of the Devil's sophisms, which alleges that one can comply with his behests for a limited period in order safely to defy him afterwards. Little by little, however, I began to lessen the tale of years to be spent in Mammon's service, and to antedate my happy emancipation from business and New York.

Two circumstances did much to hasten this process towards my release. Although, as I have said, I was not made unhappy by the work in our family warehouse, the atmosphere of that office itself grew more and more disagreeable to me. My mother's father, John Whitall, who had founded the family firm, was, outside of business, a genial, kindly old Quaker saint, the joy of his family, the dearest and kindest parent and grandparent, and one of the most public-spirited and philanthropic of the citizens of Philadelphia. But he had been, as I have said, the captain of an American sailing ship, and these captains were not famous for any excess of benevolence. Although precluded by his Quaker scruples from swearing at his men, he seems to have ruled them by other methods which had rendered blasphemy superfluous. When he left the sea, he brought with him his sea severity into that world of American business where harshness and cruelty and a slave-driving spirit were almost universal.

To these Christians, to these Quaker saints, — and saints they often were, — the notion seems never to have occurred of applying the principles of their religion to the treatment of their employees. Business was business; it was a world apart, without the slightest relation to the Heavenly Kingdom; and this merciless tradition filled the warehouse where I worked with an atmosphere which little by little I found almost stifling. Every one of the employees lived in the fear of instant dismissal, and in the hope of profiting by the disgrace of others. A heavy, blustering bully was the tyrant of the warehouse; he reigned in a glass-enclosed apartment, whither any wretch who had been caught in error was immediately summoned and subjected to a vituperation, a vilification, which reverberated loudly through the office, and was listened to by the other wretches with malignant joy and hope. "And it's in this ogre's kingdom," my soul would whisper, "that you mean to go on living! And the success you hope for is to be changed into some such ogre yourself!"

Thus the sense of malease grew, and has indeed remained with me so vividly that I never meet a rich, successful business American without some slight speculation about the bones he has crushed and the wretches he has eaten. These experiences have given me a certain dislike for the whole iron economic system upon which our civilization is founded — a dislike, however, which I must admit is by no means strong enough to make me forgo any of the pecuniary advantages which I derive from it. And anyhow I quiet my conscience — how honestly or dishonestly it would be difficult for me to say — by the reflection that I cannot think out any other economic scheme of things that would allow the human spirit to put forth fairer blossoms. The only alternatives to it seem to be Fascism and Communism, and of the prospects these offer it would be difficult to say which is the more ghastly. But that these blossoms of capitalism are nourished by something as ugly as manure seems plain enough to me when I think (as I try not to think) of our present social system, and the questionable gold which the world keeps on putting into my pockets.

The old Quakers had in their vocabulary several terms which vividly described their spiritual experiences; and among these the word "unbottoming" is one of the most picturesque. An unbottoming is the slipping away and removal of the firm basis on which the solid Quaker soul is seated; and now for me an experience of this kind was rapidly approaching. This unbottoming of mine — or, to change my metaphor, this drifting away of my soul from its familiar moorings — was not due so much to the evils of the capitalist system, for to those I was accustomed, as to something unrelated to socialism and almost incompatible with it. I became aware of a tiny breeze, a faint inspiration, a dappling of the surface of my mind by cat's-paws and tiny ripples, which took the form of the desire to write — an impulse, inherited perhaps from my dim frustrated ancestors, or a desire caught perhaps from my talks with old Walt Whitman, to endure the delicate torture of trying to express in words what I felt and saw.

To sift the sands of life for another kind of gold than the gold I was earning at the bottle warehouse began to seem to me a delicious occupation, and after my long days of work I began to spend my evenings in writing an account of a sailing expedition which I had undertaken the previous summer in a small boat from Newport to New Bedford. This I sent to the *Evening Post,* then the most literary of the New York journals, and to my amazement it was printed in its pages. I next began to write a story which was full of crude pathos, and did not possess, I now believe, the slightest literary merit. But I thought it a wonderful story, and these stolen secret joys, this foretaste of what has been since the delight and torture of my life, made me turn away with more persistence from the den of business to peep through that window which my cousin had smashed before my panic-stricken eyes. Outside was Europe, and golden leisure, long tranquil days of writing, while inside, my business stool seemed to be slipping away beneath me, and even the partners' seat, which had been the object of my ambition, began to seem a dull and cruel throne.

In the summer of 1887 my father and mother and younger sister returned from Europe, where they had spent the winter, and where at least the female members of my family had been haunted at times, I think, by a certain pity for my fate, imprisoned as I was in that New York workhouse, while they were enjoying themselves abroad. To them on their return I revealed the desire for freedom which had grown upon me; they were shocked at first, but soon joined in sympathy with my aspirations, and we began to plot together against my father, for without money from his pocket my emancipation could be nothing beyond a dream. But in every family that I have known the men are no match for the female members, who have learned how to lead these unreasonable tyrants by the nose. My mother was altogether on my side. Indeed, throughout her life she had held the conviction that what people really wanted to do was what they ought to do. When in her later life she came to be a sort of mother-confessor to the many people who used to come to her for advice in their perplexities, her advice was always, she told us, for them to do the thing they really and seriously wanted to do.

This advice she justified by the Bible text, "It is God that worketh in you both to will and to do," and "will" should be interpreted as "want," she contended, in this context. "But surely, Mother," we sometimes protested, "this is dangerous advice to give to people!" "Well," she would answer, "our Heavenly Father knows the kind of advice I give, so if He sends people to me it must be because He wants them given this advice. Besides, children," she would add, "people always in the end do what they want to do, and they might as well do it with a good conscience."

I remember once when she was full of years, and famous for her religious teachings, that a party of schoolgirls from some pious school in Philadelphia visited Oxford, and the teacher who conducted the party wrote to my mother, who was then living at Iffley, to say that it would be a privilege for the little flock of maidens to have a sight of this venerable Quaker saint, and hear from her own lips a few pious words. The permission was granted;

the schoolgirls assembled on the spacious lawn outside our house, and I wheeled my mother out in her bath chair to address them. The spectacle of all these good young girls, being prepared, as my mother knew, for lives of self-sacrifice as daughters, or as wives of American business husbands — somehow this spectacle banished from the old lady's mind the admonition she had intended for them, and when she opened her lips I was considerably surprised to hear her say, "Girls, don't be too unselfish."

"Surely, Mother," I remonstrated with her afterwards, "when those girls go home their pious relations will be dreadfully shocked by what thee said."

"Yes," she replied gayly, "yes, I dare say it will make them grind their teeth."

My mother, therefore, believing as she did that people should do the thing on which their hearts were really set, was completely on my side in my desire to leave the family business. My younger sister proved a useful ally, and steps therefore were taken to cir-

[157]

cumvent my father. The ground was carefully prepared. My father's grievances against his partners in the management of the family business were artfully exploited, and at last a careful trap was laid. My father was encouraged to expatiate on the hopes he had been forced to sacrifice when entering on his own business career; much sympathy was shown for the indignities to which he felt he had been subjected by his partners; his dislike of the harsh traditions of the firm was called up to his recollection; I was asked to describe my experiences in the New York warehouse, my subjection to its bullying manager was dwelt on, the years in which I must remain in that subjection dismally calculated; the sadness of spending my youth thus alone, thus enslaved, thus separated from my family was touched on, and then, as by a sudden impulse, I was asked to read my story. My poor father was moved by its crude pathos; his vanity and pride in his children made him perceive in it a quite nonexistent literary merit; and then when he was thus moved, thus worked

[158]

on, thus stirred like a puppet by familiar strings, the great project of my leaving the business and devoting myself to literature was, in all its horror and splendor, finally disclosed.

My father took on as all fathers do and should do on like occasions. What? To throw away this golden plum ready for my plucking, to abandon the opportunity of making a fortune, to go and live in poverty abroad when I might be making money in my native country, was a piece of folly, a kind of midsummer madness to which he could never, never (my mother smiled at this familiar word) give his paternal assent. Next he took up the theme of pathos: had he not toiled and travailed and indeed sacrificed his life for my future? Had not that been the one consolation, the one hope, which had cheered him? And was it now to be brutally suggested that this was to be taken from him, and this bright star to be dimmed forever? Was he, the indefatigable toiler of the family, to be left desolate and disappointed, with no fair expectation to cheer his declining years?

[159]

My father was possessed, as I have said, of an extraordinary gift of eloquence; I myself was really moved by this outburst, and almost persuaded to abandon so cruel a project; but my mother, who had long since learned to deafen her ears to my father's periods, soon brought us back to a truer sense of things. The business, she said, was after all the business of *her* family; it was owing to his marriage to her that my father had been made a partner in it: if I wished to abandon it, it was principally her concern. Should her brother and her nephews feel that I had put an affront upon them by abandoning the family business, she, as well as my father, must bear the blame.

This was the deft pulling of a potent string, for my father had no love for my mother's family, who had ignored what he considered his immense services to the firm, and who always treated him, he thought, as an outsider. Now, when it was his intention to retire from the business, to withdraw at the same time his son as if worthy of a nobler fate — this began to dawn upon his dramatic imagination as a splendid gesture. He was, moreover, to do him justice, an affectionate father, and full of kindly impulses; and thus caught, thus entrapped, he soon yielded, declaring that if I wanted to play the fool he would not oppose me — would indeed assist me by providing the necessary funds. He offered me a good allowance, or, if I preferred it, the meagre sum of twenty-five thousand dollars, with which I could buy an annuity that would last me all my life.

Inspired either by some premature knowledge of human nature, or more likely by a hint from my mother, I chose the capital sum. The more generous allowance offered by my father he would certainly sooner or later have felt himself forced to withdraw. Being of an impulsive and sanguine nature, he plunged into speculations in which the fortune he had acquired in business entirely disappeared. The canny Philadelphia Quakers unloaded on him a mass of shares in worthless silver mines which never paid a penny; and, when he was reduced to live upon the fortune inherited from his own father, of which, being trust money, only the life income was his, the fact that he could not lay his hands on my annuity became to him the source of a very grave grievance, but to me of unmitigated freedom. It carried me through Oxford, it enabled me to spend years in Paris, in Italy, and in an old house in Sussex. I lived on it, in fact, very happily, for nearly thirty years.

In the choice then presented for my decision between slavery in an office with the prospect of ultimate wealth, and poverty with immediate freedom, any other decision than the one I made would, it seems to me now, have been real madness, nor have I ever once, for the fraction of a minute, felt for it the least regret. For money I by no means profess a reckless disregard. But while I think it almost impossible to exaggerate the misery of pennilessness, and the degradation it involves, my experience of life has taught me to believe that, with the firm foundation of a small fixed income, money in excess of this is peculiarly subject to the law of diminishing returns. I have been both poor and comparatively rich in the course of my existence; I have associated with both poor and rich people; but, given the satisfaction of one's simple needs, I have found that, from the point of view of human happiness, the possession or absence of wealth makes very little difference — that, in fact, my poor acquaintances have been, on the whole, happier than the rich ones.

If, however, the good things of this world which wealth can purchase have come my way, I have enjoyed them, as I have enjoyed such little scraps of literary or worldly success as fate has allotted to me. But my motto has always been the wise one of Aristippus of Cyrene, ἔχω, οὐκ ἔχομαι, *habeo, non habeor*, or, to translate it into idiomatic English, "I am taken by these things, but they do not take me in," and to sacrifice one's life for them seems to me absurd.

But if my choice of poverty on this occasion was, I feel, a wise one, I also feel that it was something like madness for my father to offer it to me as he did. I had shown no particular love of study, no intellectual brilliance of any kind; my mental development was slow and backward, and the one story I had written, though it moved my father, was surely a most flimsy basis on which to build any hopes for literary success.

Nevertheless I left the New York warehouse without misgivings, and after a few months in Philadelphia we all sailed for Europe and the unknown. This was for both my father and myself our ultimate jaunt across the Atlantic. Our family had been gazing for long across the ocean. They had crossed it for religious motives; and when those motives ceased to exist, they had no reason for remaining in a land in which they were essentially aliens. Like so many English families settled on the Eastern coast of America, they had really remained in England all the time. The Burlington families were almost all Royalists, and I think we sailed with the ghostly blessings of all those other book-loving, poverty-stricken Smiths from an America to which they had been exiled for so long.

6

Oxford

MY FLIGHT from America occurred in 1888. My sister Mary was by that time married and settled in London, and her barrister husband insisted with great emphasis that I should be transferred without delay to what was, in his opinion, the only nursing home of reasonable thought and noble ambition — in fact, to Balliol College. There the spirit of T. H. Green and of Arnold Toynbee was still potent, and there the great Benjamin Jowett still lived and reigned. This had all been happily arranged, and the change from America to England, from a New York countinghouse to Oxford, seemed to me a piece of flawless good fortune. But there is a flaw, unluckily, as Emerson pointed out, in everything God has made; and I am inclined to believe now, as I muse in retrospect on these events of fifty years ago, that two slight incidents, though I saw no significance in them at the time, might without superstition be regarded as the first faint foreshadowings of the tiny rift which was destined to flaw a little the felicity of my residence in England.

Both are trivial matters, both absurd in character, the first hardly worth mentioning at all. I had reached London in advance of my luggage; my father and I were to dine the evening of our arrival with Lord and Lady Mount Temple in their great house in Stanhope Gate, and I appeared in those stately halls, at what was my first London dinner party, in dress clothes hired for the evening. My second false step was one the gravity of which Oxford men will appreciate — indeed, I shrink from mentioning it, even at the distance of fifty years. I was to travel to Oxford the next day to interview Benjamin Jowett, and I performed the journey by the London-Midland railway from Euston Station with a change of trains at Bletchley — an unheard-of method of approach, which is nevertheless given in the railway guide as an alternative to the swift and direct journey by the Great Western from Paddington. Since the distances and prices were almost identical, how was I to know the gigantic error of the route I chose?

The great Jowett, who had of course no notion that I came from Euston, received me kindly; the entrance examination to Balliol was, I must think, made easy for me, and I was taken at once into the pleasant household of A. L. Smith, later the Master of Balliol, to prepare for that examination to the University, or "Smalls," which no personal favor could modify or make easy. The little smattering of Latin and Greek which I acquired in America had faded from my mind; I was forced to begin again with the Greek alphabet. But I was anxious to learn, my tutor had a real genius for teaching, and in about three months' time I acquired that minimum of classical learning which was then necessary for admission to the University, and took up my residence in Balliol. I see myself as being at that time an easy, pleasant, well-meaning, plausible youth, older in years than my English comrades (for I was twenty-three), but in mind and education much cruder than almost any of them, though they were young and crude enough. I was the only or almost the only American in Oxford; for it was long before the great invasion had begun. I was liked, or at any rate I was kindly tolerated.

Jowett, as is well known, was the victim all his life of an absurd social shyness, a shyness he diffused about him like a kind of terror. To this I was, however, immune. I claim no credit for my lack of becoming awe; it was part of my American simplicity, and I can recall with a kind of amazement those dinner parties of his to which he would ask a few undergraduates to meet the distinguished guests who so often stayed with him. There, with their wives, were Cabinet Ministers who could face a howling House of Commons but could not face the Master;

[168]

famous travelers who had looked on danger
with unflinching eyes but who now were
paralyzed with shyness: all were as frightened of the Master as he was terrified of
them, all sat tongue-tied as in a nightmare.
It was very odd; but what seems to me now
the oddest feature of these occasions is the
fact that I was there, an undergraduate, a
clerk released not many months before from
a New York office, monopolizing the conversation. Among all those eminent people the
only words which were heard were often
spoken in my transatlantic accent. But being
young, and inexperienced in the world, I
regarded situations as simple which were full
in fact of complications; hating to see people
uncomfortable and embarrassed, I wanted
to help them to feel at ease. My host must
have been grateful to me, as he kept asking me
to his parties. I remember once how, when I
stood looking across the chasm which yawned
in his drawing-room between his London
guests and the undergraduates invited in
after dinner, I saw some London acquaint-

ances of mine and stepped across the gulf to greet them, and how the Master gave little me a pat on the back and murmured, "That 's a brave young gentleman."

But the state of society I am now describing must, I think, have vanished long ago. Eminent Englishmen now meet (except, perhaps, in royal circles) without undue embarrassment or shyness; since the death of Lord Kitchener I doubt if there is anyone who can make them shake in their shoes; and certainly the American accent is familiar, if not too familiar, to them all.

Who were the eminent personages I met at the Master's dinner parties? That they were large and shy is almost all I remember about them; I was too ignorant of contemporary life in England to attach much meaning to their names. They have faded from my memory with the exception of Lord Dufferin, of whom Harold Nicolson has just written a delightful portrait. I have a reason, somewhat beneath the dignity of history, to remember this ex-Viceroy of India, this ex-

Governor-General of Canada, who was at the time, I believe, British Ambassador in France. On arriving at the Master's I was presented to him and to his wife, who happened to make a gesture which struck me as rather odd. I paid, however, but little attention to it, as the Marquis immediately drew me apart and began talking to me in that manner full of fascination for which he was justly famous. I was naturally flattered by the way I had been singled out and drawn aside from the company upon which he turned his back, until I noticed that while he talked he was busy adjusting his costume. The odd gesture of the Marchioness had plainly been an agreed signal of a misplaced ambassadorial button which it was her high concern to put right.

Jowett not only asked me to his dinner parties, but invited me also to stay with him in his Malvern cottage. I only knew him, of course, in his old age; his work was over, he was enjoying a deserved repose after the

[171]

efforts and battles of his earlier career, and the worldly, disillusioned old man was by no means an inspiration to earnest youth. He had known so many idealists; he had been an idealist himself, and the gospel he preached had changed by now into a gospel of wet blanket. Aspirations expressed in his hearing met with no encouragement. "People are seldom better employed than in earning their own living" was a favorite aphorism of his. I remember the experience of a Balliol contemporary of mine whose ambition it was to devote himself to the pursuit of Truth. His mother, perplexed by this odd notion of her offspring, came to Oxford and took her son with her to consult the Master on the project. The youth stammered out with the enthusiasm of youth this ideal of a dedicated life, like Spinoza's. Jowett listened, looking like an old pink and white parrot. There was then a pause, in which mother and son waited anxiously for his verdict, which was: "You can get it up to £900 a year, perhaps, but no more than that."

Taking essays to read to Jowett, as in groups of two or three we used to take them, was a terrifying but also a most amusing experience. He would listen with his head cocked on one side, ready to peck at any fine sentiments or fine writing; and it was his favorite device to pretend that he had not heard the offending passage. "Read that again," he would request, in his squeaky voice; and then would come his comment. I remember once, when Macaulay was the subject of the week's essay, hearing a Scottish scholar of the college begin with a strong Scottish accent, "It is strange that anyone should have read so much and thought so little. It is strange that anyone should have done so much and lived so little." I thought this beginning full of promise, but Jowett, after insisting on its being read twice again, squeaked, "That sentence has no meaning; I must ask you to write your essay again from the very beginning." But once, rumor said, the Master had been completely nonplused; an undergraduate had begun his essay with the

[173]

sentence, "All social reformers, from Socrates and Jesus Christ to Bradlaugh and Annie Besant" (best known at that time as advocates of atheism and birth control). "Read that again," snapped Jowett; it was read again, it was read three times, and then — the Master said nothing.

I grew really fond of Jowett, though he fell far short of my priggish approbation. Any earnest student who made the slightest slip was severely punished by him, while the drunken escapade of some rowdy aristocrat would meet with the mildest of reproofs. It was perhaps part of this mellow naughtiness of his that he seemed inclined to encourage my avowed intention of devoting myself to the fine art of writing. It was an aspiration he had never before encountered; he had perhaps — who knows? — a secret sympathy with it, for he was a writer of admirable prose himself. Anyhow, he knew that such an ideal was absolutely not catching, and I dare say he was aware that the Balliol dons who were entrusted with my education would be annoyed

by any such notion; and Jowett did not in
the least mind annoying the Dons of Balliol.

But these Dons of Balliol, these "Greats"
tutors who supervised my work for the
Schools, though they were infinitely courteous and painstaking, had much more serious
reasons for disliking me (as I am sure they did
dislike me) than any fantastic desire of mine
to be a writer. My mind, though they may
have dimly hoped at first that it could be
coached to win First-Class honors for the
college, must have seemed to them sadly
lacking, as indeed it was, in discipline and
training. I think that by a kind of instinct
they realized that I had come to Oxford from
Euston, and that no subsequent drilling could
repair the error of this Midland journey.

Sir Walter Raleigh describes in one of his
letters a paper read in his research class at
Oxford by a Rhodes Scholar. "It was empty,
magniloquent, abstract, flatulent, pretentious, confused, and sub-human. I could have
wept salt tears. But I could n't do anything
else; the young man wanted a clean heart

[175]

and a new spirit, not a little top-dressing."
All these adjectives would, I am sure, apply
to the essays I used to read to these long-
suffering tutors. They must have felt acutely
my need of the clean heart and a new spirit;
and so conscientiously did they attempt to
supply me with them that now for the very
first time in my life I was, as we say, "up
against it" — this was my first contact with
real education, with the standards of real
scholarship and thought.

The Oxford School of *Litterae humaniores* —
or "Greats," as it is called — seems to my
mature judgment the best scheme of education that I have ever heard of. It is based
upon an accurate knowledge of Greek and
Latin texts, especially the texts of Plato and
Aristotle and Thucydides and Tacitus, and
the subjects studied in it are the eternal prob-
lems of thought, of conduct, and of social
organization. These are discussed, not by
means of contemporary catchwords, but by
translating them back into another world
and another language. Nor could anything

[176]

be more profitable from the pupil's point of view than the way in which this scheme of education was carried on. The student would prepare a paper on some special subject, and go with it, generally alone, and read it to his tutor, who would then discuss it and criticize it at length; or a group of two or three would meet in the tutor's room for a kind of Socratic discussion of some special point. These discussions were carried on much in the spirit of the Socratic dialogues; and the Socratic irony and assumed ignorance of the instructors, their deferential questions, as if the pupil were the teacher and they the learners, was a method which I found it hard at first to understand.

I remember, for instance, in reading a paper to Nettleship, I mentioned the distinction between form and matter. "Excuse me for interrupting you," Nettleship said, "but this distinction you make, though it is no doubt most important, is one that I find a little difficult to grasp. If it is not troubling you too much, it would be a real kindness if you would try to explain it to me."

"Oh, it 's quite simple," I answered patronizingly. "There 's the idea, say, in a poem, and there 's the way in which it is expressed."

Nettleship still seemed puzzled. "Could you give me an instance?" he pleaded.

"Oh, nothing easier," I answered. "Take the lines, for instance, when Lovelace says,

> I could not love thee, Dear, so much,
> Loved I not Honour more.

Now he might have said, 'I could n't be nearly so fond of you, my dear, if I did n't care still more for my reputation.' The form, you see, is very different in both these sentences, but the subject of them — what they mean — is exactly the same."

Nettleship seemed greatly discouraged. "I 'm afraid," he said, "I can't see that the meaning of the two sentences is the same. I 'm afraid I 'm very stupid; but to me they seem to say quite different things."

He was, I thought, curiously stupid; but in my patient attempt to make my meaning clearer to him a dim suspicion began to waken in me that perhaps it was not Nettleship but I myself who was playing the part of the fool in this dialogue.

The Oxford School of Greats, and the Oxford tutorial system, which had been perfected by Jowett, and was seen at its very best in Balliol College, were exactly what I needed to knock out of me my pretentious superficiality; and if I have to any degree attained a "clean heart and new spirit," I owe it to these years of careful tuition and personal guidance at Balliol. Yet I cannot but feel that this system of personal tuition involved an intolerable waste of fine material, and that it was a fantastic, almost a wicked thing that hours and hours of the time of men like Nettleship and Abbott and the other Greats tutors should have been devoted to the culture of an intellect so raw and crude as mine.

Nor can I believe that this patient, persistent instruction and spoon-feeding of individuals is the proper function of university teachers, or that, to the best minds already well grounded at school, such additional schoolmastering can be really beneficial. Universities should, it seems to me, be organized, not for the purpose of educating the second-rate and stupid, for transforming at infinite expense of labor the ears of sows into some poor semblance of silk purses, but for the enlightenment and development of the keenest intelligences, for the encouragement by example of original research. Daring and original minds are cramped and injured by being always led in strings and fed on pap which has been carefully prepared for them. They should be allowed to make their profitable mistakes; and, above all, their spirits should be kindled by contact with original scholars and masters of first-hand learning.

To any such ideal the hard-worked college tutor, who had generally begun tutoring the moment he ceased to be a pupil, could have, of course, no chance of attaining. Naturally he tended to depreciate those who attempted to achieve this ideal, and he had not far to look for them. There existed at Oxford, in a kind of shadowy world, a whole body of university

professors, men of original learning and research, who were generally appointed from
outside, and who lectured on the same subjects as the college tutors. But of all this I
had not the slightest notion. My only inti-
mation of it was when I was calling one day
on the Regius Professor of Modern History
(whom I had met traveling in Sicily) and
heard him tell his parlormaid to run over to
his lecture room across St. Giles and see if
there were any auditors assembled. In this
case, the Professor told me, he would be compelled to attend himself. The maid soon
brought back the accustomed news that the
lecture room was completely empty, and so
we were enabled to have our tea in peace.

My host's predecessor, the great historian
Stubbs, had undergone much the same neglect when he came to lecture in Oxford. The
trouble was that professors would lecture on
things that interested them, rather than provide information which might prove useful
in those examinations in which the colleges
competed fiercely with each other, and no

college more fiercely than my own. Indeed, it might have easily happened in Oxford at this period (I don't know how it would be now) that the greatest authority in the world might give a lecture on his special subject, and not one of those tutors who taught that subject, or those undergraduates who were engaged in its study, would find it worth his while to attend the lecture. Certainly any desire to do so would have been seriously frowned upon in Balliol, as being likely to interfere with that triumph of Balliol over other colleges which was held before our eyes as the highest and noblest of university aims.

Balliol College, drunk with its triumph in the university examinations, had made success of this kind its glory and ideal, and the immense importance of gaining a First and thus helping to defeat and disconcert and keep down all rival colleges was continually impressed upon us. I remember receiving a dim impression of this passion when I read an essay on some special point in Roman history to my tutor. I had taken an unusual interest in this subject, which I had chosen for myself, and I had read and thought with special thoroughness about it. I was proud of my essay, and my tutor gave it unusual praise, in which praise I was conscious of the mingling of a curious malease. "Yes," he said, "this is an excellent piece of work, the best work of yours I have seen; if all your work were of this quality you might get a First, and do honor to your college. But I 'm afraid that, after all, your time has been wasted. That question was asked by the examiners last year."

This ideal of winning Firsts in examinations for the glory of Balliol was so impressed upon me that, though I have little college patriotism remaining, and an Oxford First has lost all its glory in my eyes, I still study in *The Times* the examination lists and count up the Firsts achieved by the various colleges, and rejoice when, as almost always happens, I find that Balliol still maintains its old preëminence.

All the same, this spirit of competition between one college and another seems to me

now more schoolboyish and absurd than
most forms of patriotic sentiment, and I find
it difficult to understand how serious and
noble men like the Balliol dons could have
been inspired by such childish ambitions, and
done all they could — and they could do
much — to inspire others with them. Of
course the rational, judicious hatred I entertain for our rival university, Cambridge,
being founded on reason and free from prejudice of any kind, is quite another matter,
and should not be so much as mentioned
here.

The other ideal strongly impressed upon
Balliol undergraduates was the duty of getting on in the world; and indeed triumph in
examinations was above all praised as the
first step on the path to more important
triumphs. It has been said of Jowett that he
united with high moral and religious serious-
ness the plain determination that his pupils
should not fail of mundane distinction; and,
naughty as he may have become in other

ways, at worldly success he never mocked.
There was much glorification on college occasions of the Balliol men who had achieved
high honors and positions. College gaudies
were gaudy indeed with the litany of glorious
names recited on these occasions — names of
viceroys, archbishops, cabinet ministers, even
prime ministers who were sons of Balliol, and
who not infrequently would return as grateful sons to their Alma Mater and shed their
lustre upon the college whence they had first
winged their flights. To tell the truth, I came
in the end to find these entertainments rather
cloying to my taste; and though the roll call
of Balliol names has grown with the years
even more illustrious, I am inspired with no
desire to listen to it. I am glad that members
of my college have performed noble services
in the world, and have been nobly rewarded
by a grateful nation; but loud proclamations
of these achievements and reiterated college
boastings I find, to tell the truth, rather bor-
ing. I should more joyfully attend a gaudy
for the black sheep of the college, the scape-

graces and ne'er-do-wells; and if men of literary distinction like Matthew Arnold or Swinburne, or others famous for scholarly research, had been praised on these occasions (which never happened), I should have listened with greater interest.

The word "Research" as a university ideal had, indeed, been ominously spoken in Oxford by that extremely cantankerous person, Mark Pattison, some years ago; but the notion of this ideal, threatening as it did to discredit the whole tutorial and examinational system which was making Oxford into the highest of high schools for boys, was received there with anger and contempt. In Balliol, the birthplace and most illustrious home of this great system, it was regarded with especial scorn. If the prize fellowships and the fellowships at All Souls were to be no longer regarded as the legitimate reward of those who had won First Classes in the Schools; if the means they provided were not to be spent in helping ambitious young men on the first rungs of the ladder of worldly success, but used, as Mark

[186]

Pattison's ill-mannered supporters suggested, in the maintenance of researchers, ambitious of the fame of scholars, would not the whole tutorial system be deprived of one of its important features, and the university endowments be seriously abused? This ideal of endowment for research was particularly shocking to Benjamin Jowett, the great inventor of the tutorial system which it threatened. I remember once, when staying with him at Malvern, inadvertently pronouncing the ill-omened word. "Research!" the Master exclaimed. "Research!" he said. "A mere excuse for idleness; it has never achieved, and will never achieve, any results of the slightest value." At this sweeping statement I protested, whereupon I was peremptorily told, if I knew of any such results of value, to name them without delay. My ideas on the subject were by no means profound, and anyhow it is difficult to give definite instances of a general proposition at a moment's notice. The only thing that came into my head was the recent discovery, of which I had read somewhere, that on striking a patient's kneecap sharply he would give an involuntary kick, and that by the vigor or lack of vigor of this "knee jerk," as it is called, a judgment could be formed of his general state of health.

"I don't believe a word of it," Jowett replied. "Just give my knee a tap."

I was extremely reluctant to perform this irreverent act upon his person, but the Master angrily insisted, and the undergraduate could do nothing but obey. The little leg reacted with a vigor which almost alarmed me, and must, I think, have considerably disconcerted that elderly and eminent opponent of research.

I fear that I have succumbed to my love of irony in writing of the tutorial system and Balliol and the Balliol dons. In all sincerity, however, I feel that I cannot be too grateful to Nettleship, to Strachan Davidson, to Forbes and Abbott, for the unstinted trouble they took to give me the new heart I needed. For all the purposes they cared for, I was almost

certainly useless: I could not be expected to
add to the glory of Balliol either in the Schools
or in the world of great affairs; and yet hour
after hour they tutored me and listened, I
will not say unweariedly, but at any rate without any manifestation of weariness, to my essays. Though I feel sure they did not like me,
no sign of this ever appeared in the beautiful
courtesy with which I was always treated by
them.

Balliol gave me much, gave me some ele-
ments of real education, some tincture of the
classics; from the spirit of high endeavor fos-
tered in the college I was stimulated to feel
that life was an opportunity for achievement,
that there were laurels to be gathered and
garlands to be run for. But the civic garlands
which were prized in Balliol were not really
objects of my ambition; I still wished to culti-
vate the art of letters, and no such notion was
encouraged in that college. Indeed, save for
a mild appreciation of music, there was at
that time no interest in any of the arts in
Balliol. The Master and Fellows had de-

stroyed almost all the antique beauty of the college, building upon its ruins a hideous castle of the Philistines; and it was in this castle, where young Philistines were being trained to go forth and conquer and rule the kingdoms of the world, it was in this castle that I dwelt — high up, in fact, in one of its battlemented towers.

But to me, dwelling thus among the children of this world, and toiling with them for that success which leads to worldly advancement; to me, enmeshed as I was in all the social, political, and philanthropic interests of my companions, there floated through the Oxford air, there drifted over the college walls, a voice, whispering, as in the delicate cadences of the Oxford bells, enchantments very unlike anything I heard in the college lecture rooms or chapel. If you would save your soul, the voice seemed to whisper, if you would discover that personal and peculiar sense of life which is your most precious endowment, you must practise and perfect a habit of discrimination; amid all you hear and see you must choose whatever is relevant and significant to you, and only that, rejecting with equal sincerity everything that is not really yours — all the interests you catch from others, all the standards and beliefs and feelings which are imposed on you by the society and the age you live in. Watch above all, the voice admonished me in its grave accents, for those special moments of illumination within, or of visible delight from the world around you, which seem to set free the spirit for a moment. Not to discriminate these visitations of beauty, not thus to respond to them, is, the voice admonished me, on this short day of frost and sunshine, to sleep before evening.

Thus from not far off in space, but across a whole world, as it were, of thought, the voice of Walter Pater reached me, reached me perhaps alone among my companions. It was, however, only through his books that I knew him, for I never met this famous author, who was by no means famous in Oxford at this time, being disregarded there and held of no

account. Edmund Gosse once told me that
when the memorial to Shelley was installed
in University College, and a great gathering
of the famous writers and eminent intellectuals of the land were assembled to be present
at the unveiling of this monument, he himself
had gone to Oxford and had suggested that
Walter Pater should give him luncheon. Pater
entertained him with his usual grave amen-
ity; and when luncheon was finished, and
Gosse suggested that it was time to join the
others who were to be present at the cere-
mony, Pater told him where to go, but said
that he himself could not accompany him as
he was not among those who had received an
invitation to attend.

In Balliol, indeed, the name of Pater was
known, but it was only mentioned with contempt. Pater had been an early pupil of
Jowett's; they had read Plato together; and
I have always believed, though I have no
proofs to give, that it was Jowett who had
advised Pater to give up the writing of verse,
to which he was greatly addicted, and try to

become a writer of good prose. But when this effort resulted in the publication of Pater's *Renaissance*, Jowett took alarm at once.

While all melts under our feet, we may well catch at any exquisite passion, or any contribution to knowledge that seems by a lifted horizon to set the spirit free for a moment, or any stirring of the senses, strange dyes, and curious odours, or work of the artist's hands, or the face of one's friend. . . .
To burn always with this hard, gemlike flame, to maintain this ecstasy, is success in life.

So Pater chanted from Brasenose in his magic rhythms, but his view of things was not acceptable in Balliol. To maintain an ecstasy, to burn with a hard gemlike flame, was by no means the Balliol conception of triumphant achievement. To beat New College in the Schools, to maintain a good place on the river, to win All Souls Fellowships and brilliant places in the Civil Service and high official honors, was more consonant with their ideal. No doubt this was the wiser view; no doubt the efficiency, wisdom, and justice which on the whole rule the counsels of the British Empire are in no inconsiderable part due to the moral, manly influence of Balliol.

It is not surprising, therefore, that not long before I went to Balliol the Master had felt himself called upon to mark, in an almost public manner, his disapprobation of Pater and all his ways; and it was only much later, when Pater published his wise and beautiful book on *Plato and Platonism*, that Jowett modified the harshness of his earlier judgment.

For the rest, I shared in that Oxford life which, in its setting of old colleges and gardens and little rivers, is surely the happiest and most enchanting life that is possible to young mortals. A taste of Paradise, a bit of the old golden world — so it seemed to me after my emancipation from that ogre's den in America. I had not known that life could hold such happiness, such enchanting talks and friendships, such kindness and good-fellowship; and I drank to the full from the

[194]

enchanted cup. My literary ambitions, if they could be called ambitions, though not forgotten, were in abeyance for the time; my business was to get an education; and though I was acquainted with the budding authors who were at Oxford with me, — Lionel Johnson, Laurence Binyon, and Max Beerbohm, — I did not become intimate with any of them; I was contented with the society I found in my own college. This society was made up, for the most part, of young men who belonged to the Whig political families, the Russells, the Carlisle Howards, and the Peels, who were destined to careers in the world of politics. I too became engaged in political activities; I used to speak at village meetings and work for Liberal candidates at by-elections; I joined the Oxford Charity Organization Committee; I organized meetings for temperance and social propaganda; and I think I was best known in Oxford as belonging to the not very estimable type of social reformer who combines extreme democratic views with no very pronounced dislike of the society of lords. In the dim anecdotal atmosphere of old-fashioned Oxford common rooms, where stories are elaborately related over the port wine and the walnuts, I have reason to believe that dialogues were invented between me and two American young ladies who were supposed to be studying in Oxford, in which perambulators were referred to as "push-buggies," and spittoons were much discussed under the name of "cuspidors."

My political activities gave rise to at least one story which I should like to think still survives — I know that it did survive till very recently. During the election of 1892 a Balliol acquaintance of mine contested for Parliament and won the Woodstock division of Oxfordshire; and I, with several other enthusiastic Balliol Liberals, took lodgings in that rural district and canvassed and held meetings for our candidate. His opponent was an older Balliol man, Lyttelton Gell by name, who had rooms in the college (in what capacity I don't remember) and also a handsome residence on Headington Hill, above

Oxford, where he dwelt in some state with his wife, a niece of George Brodrick, the Warden of Merton, and daughter of the Lord Midleton of the time. They were at home to Balliol men on Sundays, the first Sunday of the term being devoted (so the mocking Russells used to say) to members of the aristocracy, the second Sunday to the sons of gentlemen, and the third to Americans and Jews. On these third Sundays, I was sometimes a guest. The Lyttelton Gells were friendly if somewhat pompous persons; the connection of Mrs. Gell with the peerage was, perhaps, a little overstressed in a place like Oxford, where such relationships are not frequent. Above all, her title of "Honourable," always a difficult title for the uninitiated to handle, — or rather to let alone, — presented certain possibilities of error into which I was supposed to have fallen. During the election it was related that I was seen in glimpses like the Scholar Gypsy wandering through the landscape at the head of a band of Balliol radicals, bearing a banner with the strange device: —

[197]

To Hell, to Hell
With the Honourable Gell.

Dining in Oxford not long ago, I heard this anecdote told by an elderly don who had no notion that I was the hero of it; and if this ghost of my undergraduate days still, like the Scholar Gypsy, survives, may I not boast *non omnis moriar?* Should this story still run through Oxford halls, I shall owe to it, even without the aid of the grave Glanvill and the elegiac Matthew Arnold, a more enduring remembrance than any I might earn by a feat I had been long contemplating. I had reached Oxford by the untraveled route from Euston; my ambition all along had not been to win the rewards it offered — not to conquer Oxford, but to write a book about it.

7

Paris

TO WRITE about Oxford! But first of all I must learn to write — that was now the task before me. Oxford had been celebrated by Matthew Arnold in "Thyrsis" and "The Scholar Gypsy"; Bablock Hythe, the river above Godstow, Cumnor and Fyfield and the road to Hinksey, the skirts of Bagley Wood — all had won their place, and I believe their permanent place. in poetry.

But what had been written of Oxford in prose that one cared to remember? There was Lamb's essay on "Oxford in the Vacation"; there was Matthew Arnold's famous passage about the home of "lost causes, and forsaken beliefs, and unpopular names, and impossible loyalties," and his description of the sight of Newman gliding into the pulpit of St. Mary's,

[199]

and then breaking the silence in "the most entrancing of voices." Then there was Newman's own mention of the snapdragon growing on the walls of Trinity College, and of the spires of Oxford, seen after many years as he traveled in the train to Birmingham. These passages lingered in my imagination, but they were brief and casual; why should n't I try to repay my debt to Oxford by attempting to write a longer book about it? Would n't it be pleasant even to fail in such an attempt? But the art of writing such a book as it should be written was not to be learned at Oxford. The *Cursus honorum* that led upwards from one academic and worldly success to another was not the way that led to any achievement of this kind. The example of my prophet, however, seemed to justify the hope that somewhere, somehow, I might possibly create for myself the talent necessary for my purpose. For Pater's accomplishment was in no way due to what we call genius, but to perfected talent — was indeed a classical example of such a talent, created by almost infinite artifice and pains. It was talent, moreover, for writing prose; and with my delight in the beauty of English prose, — the "fine writing," as it is derisively called, of our older authors, — I welcomed his declaration that to limit prose to mere lucidity was no more than a narrow and puritanical restriction. It was and could be, he said, an instrument of many stops, musical, picturesque, intimate, and fervid; and, thus conceived, it was the appropriate and most promising medium for the rendering of modern life. All this was to me the most precious gospel, and when I heard that, in a group of young men who were discussing poetry, Pater had said his ambition was to shine as a writer of good prose, I rejoiced the more, since I believed that this suggestion had come from the lips of the commander of that castle of the Philistines in which I then happened to be dwelling.

Pater, deep-buried among the aborigines of Brasenose, could pursue in that uncomprehending solitude whatever moral or æsthetic purpose pleased his fancy — no one there would have the slightest inkling of his purpose. But in Balliol they were cleverer than that; they knew that I had openly professed my ambition to be a writer, that I had mocked at the examination system, declaring that none of the Oxford authors who had become famous, not Matthew Arnold or Newman or Walter Pater or Robert Bridges, had achieved First Classes in its Schools, while those stamps of mediocrity had been bestowed upon Frederic Harrison and Oscar Wilde. They knew, moreover, that I had persuaded more than one of my contemporaries to decline the membership of clubs, advantageous from a worldly point of view, to which they had been elected. Jowett was dead; rebels and mockers had no longer a patron in the college, and it was felt, and rightfully felt, that it would be well for me to betake myself elsewhere with my volumes of Pater, my French novels, and above all, perhaps, with the oil painting by Blake which I had acquired, and which was regarded by the Dons of Balliol with considerable suspicion.

Paris

Whither should I go? There was, of course, but one answer. In all the inhabited world there exists, and has existed, only one centre of disinterested artistic interest. Paris welcomes would-be artists with its urbane, heartless grace; it provides them with every facility for learning the art they will never learn to practise; it appropriates with a charming smile the savings they have brought with them, and with the same smile it watches them fade away or perish, knowing that new generations will soon appear to occupy their little hotels and lodgings. All are doomed, as Paris knows, to inevitable failure, but it goes on with its own business, remunerated and undisturbed.

Every year these art students arrive out of the darkness like flights of birds; they rejoice for brief or longer periods in the Paris sunshine, and then they disappear, and what becomes of them no one knows or cares. Do they return to their original homes, to teach art in provincial art schools and to paint the portraits of local magnates, or do they simply moulder away and die? Nobody, as I say, knows or cares.

The immense forgathering, as if drawn by some irresistible magnet, of æsthetic Americans in Paris was remarkable as a mass phenomenon; but the individuals who composed that mass, though I lived among them for a while, I did not find interesting. They had come to Paris from almost every region of my native country, at who knows what sacrifice to themselves and to their parents, to study art; but in art itself they seemed to take hardly any interest — they almost never visited the Louvre, nor did they discuss any of the great masterpieces of European painting. Their talk was all of their own or each other's pictures and of the little twopenny shows where they were to be seen on exhibition. These pictures, painted with elaborate pains, were all alike, all imitative of each other; the narrow space of their little shows was filled with a vast, an almost intolerable monotony. Most interesting among these American students I found the indomitable old ladies who, released by the happy demise of their husbands and the maturity of their children, had escaped at last, at the age of seventy, perhaps, or even eighty, to realize their dreams of studying art in Paris. But these old ladies, whom one would see seated in their prim bonnets in the art schools, industriously making drawings of huge and naked males, all painted the same picture as their young contemporaries; it was not possible to distinguish among them. And yet no generalization is ever absolutely true. From among the thousands of indistinguishable art students of our race had emerged the American Whistler, the Englishman Sickert, and the Australian Charles Conder. Of these Whistler and Conder were then living in Paris.

On leaving Oxford, I had rented for twenty pounds a year a charming apartment — three rooms looking on a great cherry tree in a little garden — in the curious, shabby, provincial, yet cosmopolitan, Montparnasse quarter of Paris, with its little shops, its vast mysterious convents, its broad boulevards close by. It so happened that Whistler had his studio almost round the corner, and I often saw him either at this studio or at the charming pavilion where he lived with his English wife in the garden of an aristocratic hotel not far off. Whistler was then engaged in what was for him the almost interminable process of painting a portrait — the subject was the Comte de Montesquieu. This nobleman (whom Proust afterwards made famous) was depicted in an aristocratic pose, standing with a fur coat on his arm, and could not be expected to give the almost innumerable sessions which Whistler demanded of his subjects; but I could be easily called in to act as his substitute in certain aspects of his appearance. I was, like him, tall and slim, and could competently stand there with what was the principal feature of the picture, the fur coat, flung across the arm. I was pleased to oblige the great painter, I was delighted to enjoy his company and watch him paint; but the task was one of the most arduous I have ever undertaken. Whistler had not the slightest pity for his subjects; art was something sacred, and the sufferings of those in its service were a matter of complete indifference to him. If, when he had finished his portraits of his sitters, they should all perish, what could that have mattered to the world? From the point of view of eternity, there is much to be said for this attitude of the artist. Of what interest or importance to us now are all their models? They are now all dust, and, as Donne would have pointed out, dust that is no longer even capable of emitting an evil odor. Why should we bother ourselves about them?

But to die in the effort to make immortal the fur coat of a stranger seemed to me a somewhat excessive sacrifice; and when I had stood until I felt I should die if I stood there longer, and would beg for a little rest or some change of position, "In a moment, in just a moment," Whistler would cheerfully answer, and then would go on painting. His method, as I observed it, was first of all to arrange his subject with incredible pains and care, so that

every detail was to his liking, and to paint it
with infinite touches and retouches; and then,
when it seemed finished and perfect in execu-
tion, to stand back, gaze at it, and cry "Ha!"
and rush at it in a kind of fury and paint the
whole thing out. It was like an actor rehears-
ing a part over and over again till he gets it
perfect; the final performance, which may take
a minute, has been preceded by many hours
of rehearsal. This was the case, I think,
even with Whistler's life-size portraits. The
actual painting of each, as we now see it, was
performed in the briefest of periods, but these
had been preceded by an almost infinite number of rehearsals.

Such at least were my reflections as I stood
till I almost dropped, bearing on my arm the
Count's fur coat, which would be painted
again and again with exquisite care in every
detail, then again and again be painted out.
But all things have an end, and at last respite
would come. Whistler would abandon his
brushes, and we would sit down to an entertainment which consisted not only in a deli-

Paris

cious luncheon, but in talk as amusing as any
I have ever heard. Whistler was not only in-
comparable as a wit (his *Gentle Art of Making
Enemies* is proof enough of that), but he had
accumulated (and I think repolished by frequent repetition) a long series of anecdotes
concerning his life in England, in which every
person of distinction, every institution of
importance with which he had come into
contact in that country, was made more
ridiculous than words can say.

Self-important people, who take themselves
seriously, have always worn for me a slightly
comic aspect, and Whistler's mockery of the
official side of English institutions I found
extremely amusing. Outside of his art I did
not regard him as a person deserving of much
estimation. The record of his quarrels is more
funny than edifying, and he was too fond of
publicity and self-advertisement for my taste.
But these failings hardly matter in a painter
who, with regard to his painting, possessed a
conscience of the utmost delicacy, and a sense
of honor surpassing all I have ever known or

heard of in what is after all perhaps the most honorable of all the arts. To do anything second-rate for money, or any kind of personal or social advantage, would never have been possible to Whistler; and though at times there was a touch in him of the loud, bar-frequenting American, his taste in matters of art was infallible and exquisite; he loved his paintings, and I think he could have told at any moment in what gallery or private collection even the most insignificant of them could be found. The paint brush was his appropriate weapon, and I remember once, when he was writing a series of outrageous letters, Mrs. Whistler's remarking that Jimmy would be all right if he could only be kept from the inkpot.

Whistler I came to know through the means of three Irish-American young women who were devoted friends of his. They were rich, were lovely, and all as good as gold. Both their parents dying suddenly, they had come to finish their education (for they were Roman Catholics) at the Sacré-Cœur in

Paris, and had then stayed on vaguely month by month, year by year, in France. They lived in a charming manner, either in their Paris apartment or in a house in the noble landscape of the lower Seine, first at Giverny (where Monet lived) and then in the little town of Vétheuil, not far off. Giverny was a village situated on a little brimming tributary of the Seine; Vétheuil stood on the banks of that noble stream itself. In each village there were enchanting little inns, and these inns were largely populated, especially in the springtime, by the young artists and writers. We all adored these ladies, who, though they were not averse to the admiration they excited, preferred to live in the freedom of maiden meditation. They were willing, however, to sit endlessly for their portraits and no better subjects could be found. The second Miss Kinsella was, I think, with her blonde beauty, her golden hair, and her expression of gentle softness, the most lovely human being I have ever seen; and Charles Conder, the quiet, handsome, and silent Australian artist, who had not the strength to resist the temptations of Paris, was invited (at my suggestion) to Giverny, and, falling in love with her at once, never really painted any other human being. She died too soon, but she still lives in the pictures he made of her amid the apple blossoms of Vétheuil, and in Whistler's portrait of her, where she stands, somewhat startled, like a forgotten princess, gazing at a fête in which she has no part.

Do I exaggerate the charm of these ladies? To prove that they are not creatures of my imagination, I will quote a letter written by Sir Walter Raleigh, after a visit they had paid to England: —

My wife and I are agreed — you do not care for us a bit. The plaguy part of the business is that we dote on you, so farewell to all hope of preserving dignity of attitude. May you never be crossed in love. Meanwhile how can we prevent your shameful escape to France?

And us with a beautiful house at that emporium of elegance and culture, Oxford, and never a day's pleasure to be had out of it, but breaking the furniture and all, because you are in a hateful little packet boat that plies for hire between Dover and Calais. O worthless world, O transitory things. And you laughing at us. Of all the ladies I have ever loved you display the least pretence of reciprocity. It was not a sincere petition of that Prince of Insincerity, Mr. Robert Burns :

> If love for love ye will not gie
> At least be pity on me shown —

but it *has* been customary nevertheless to drop a pennyworth of pity into the hat that was taken off for love's sake.

If only I knew what string to pull, to agitate your hearts. And if only I could reach it. However dark or high, it must exist. . . . But there it is — we breakfast on it, lunch on it, dine on it, see it in the glass, and in the papers ; get thin on it, pray on it, and swear on it : you don't care for us.

P.S. You know quite well we can't bear it. Tell us what to do.

The Raleighs came afterwards to Vétheuil, joining our little community there. Thither

came also D. S. MacColl, as well as other
writers and painters I might mention, and
one or two of my chosen Balliol friends. One
day I was lunching in a little restaurant in
Paris and happened to sit by two young Englishmen with whom I soon fell into conversation. We talked for a long time together
and agreed to meet again. One was Roger
Fry, with whom I formed a friendship that
lasted till his death. The other was Lowes
Dickinson. They represented the purest
strain of Cambridge Apostles, and thus was
begun a relation with the Cambridge intellectuals which was much strengthened by the
marriage, some years later, of Bertrand Rus-
sell to my younger sister. In the meantime,
however, I told Roger Fry and Dickinson of
the charms of Vétheuil and took them thither
— at least I took Roger Fry, who fell (and
fell badly) under the spell of that place and
of those ladies.

I turn to a text from Homer: Why,
Apollo asks of the great Earth-shaker, why
should we concern ourselves with human be-

ings who flourish only as the leaves flourish, and then fall forgotten to the earth? Of those who frequented Vétheuil forty years ago almost all have perished. But to be remembered, or at least to save the places and people one has cared for from being utterly forgotten, is not the least unworthy of human desires. Perhaps someone may read these pages when I am no longer living; more probably those April-blossoming days at Vétheuil will survive in Conder's pictures. I should be sorry if their petals were mingled in the unremembered dust.

All this time I was working, either at Vétheuil or in my apartment in Paris, at my book about Oxford. Youth must find its nourishment in the work of its contemporaries. Of my contemporaries Whitman had died in 1892, Pater two years later, while Matthew Arnold had preceded Pater by six years. But Flaubert, martyr as he was of the art of writing, though he had died before I went to Paris, was my saint and hero. The four volumes of his letters were like a Bible to me, and now, when I look again at the texts I marked, the old flames illuminate those pages. The true writer is a kind of priest, he says, his devotion makes him proud, and we are none of us proud enough. "But when I think of my solitude and my agonies I ask myself whether I am an idiot or a saint. But without fanaticism we can accomplish nothing worth while, and folly for folly why not choose the noblest among them?

"Genius is a gift of the Gods, but Talent is our affair; and with untiring patience one can acquire talent in the end. But why should one publish? I write for my own pleasure, as a bourgeois in his garret turns out napkin rings on his lathe. . . . The wine of art is the cause of an intoxication that knows no end. . . . Speaking with all sincerity everything is ignominy here below but art."

These are some of the sentences I copied out from Flaubert's letters. I believed them all (and, idiotic as it may seem, I still believe them).

Paris

From Flaubert's letters I turned to the writings of his nephew and disciple, Guy de Maupassant, who died when I was in Paris, and whose short stories seemed to me just the hard, poignant, accomplished masterpieces I should have liked to produce myself. To these influences must be added the thrill of beautiful modernity (and than that can anything be more thrilling?) produced by the high noon of impressionism which was just then revealing to our young, astonished eyes a new, fresh-painted world of bright sunlight and mauve trees and blue grass and blue shadows which we had never seen before.

The inevitable product of all this was a volume of short stories about Oxford, impressionist in their coloring, and matching in form the neat, accomplished construction of Maupassant. This labored, imitative, rather lifeless book was published in 1895, and of course it fell completely flat. On re-reading it the other day, however, I felt that it was not entirely devoid of merit, and that probably if it were published now, when attention is somewhat more alert in these matters, it might perhaps win at least enough success to encourage its author to proceed in a way of writing for which he had no natural vocation. If I had had a gift for writing stories no one failure would have stifled it. Still, I liked my little book, and was disappointed that it had no interest for the public. It brought me two friends, one of whom was Robert Bridges, who after reading it asked me to come to see him at Yattendon, where he was then living; the other was Phelps, the Dean of Oriel, who later became the Provost of that most charming of the little colleges in Oxford. Bridges and Phelps remained my friends till their death years later; and the other day I heard, after forty years of oblivion, my book of short stories mentioned with appreciation. It occurs to me now that this was a success more to be valued, after all, than the sale of numerous editions.

But was there not then a great lion in my path with whom it was folly to think of competing? It was just about this period that my fellow expatriate, Henry James, was writing his best short stories; and in the year my little book was published appeared the volume called *Terminations*, in which are contained three at least of his masterpieces, the "Death of the Lion," the "Coxon Fund," and the "Altar of the Dead." I sent this master, with whom I was slightly acquainted, my little book; he mislaid it in the Underground, and after some weeks he wrote a letter full of apologies in which he told me that he had procured another copy, and asked me to come and see him and talk the book over. Of course I went. Henry James was to me then but a revered master, not the friend he became afterwards, and I listened with reverent ears to what he said about my stories. His praise was kindly but tepid; I think he saw the gift for story writing was not my gift; and, as he said in another connection, although one may lie about anything else, about matters of art one does n't lie. About the profession of letters in general, the desire to do the best one could with one's pen, — and this I confessed was my ambition, — he made one remark which I have never forgotten. "My young friend," he said, "and I call you young, — you are disgustingly and, if I may be allowed to say so, nauseatingly young, — there is one thing that, if you really intend to follow the course you indicate, I cannot too emphatically insist on. There is one word — let me impress upon you — which you must inscribe upon your banner, and that," he added after an impressive pause, "that word is *Loneliness*."

8

Sussex

I RETURNED to Paris, and found that my little flat had been let to a young married couple, and the study where I had labored at my stories was now being transformed into the nursery for birth of a more normal type. The ladies at Vétheuil had also ceased to inhabit that enchanted region; Whistler had gone — who knows whither? Conder was no longer to be found in his habitual haunts; his half-imaginary engagement to the lady of Vétheuil had come to an end as vague as its beginning. In fact our little group, as always happens to such little groups, had melted away.

It so happened that at just this time an old house fell vacant not far distant from my father's house in Sussex — a gray, eighteenth-century farmhouse in a quiet place under

[221]

high hills, and among great trees and meadows. It had been, years ago, the home of one of the ironmasters who had smelted the iron in the soil of that district. They had achieved modest fortunes by this process; but the exhaustion of the oak forests around them, and still more the discovery of coal and iron ore almost side by side in Northern England, had led to the decay of this Sussex industry. Heaps of slag buried in new-grown forests, and a few beautiful old houses, once the habitations of these vanished ironmasters, were all that that old industry had left behind it.

Such a house was High Buildings. It had become a farmhouse; the farmer was now leaving, and it was to let, with its fields and gardens, for only ten pounds more than I had been paying for my rooms in Paris.

I decided to take this house. I could live there for almost nothing; a woman from the village would come daily for my modest housekeeping; the garden I could attend to myself. For the next ten years, therefore, this was my home. I had a few pleasant neighbors, and my father's house near by was full of guests all the summer. I have just been looking at one of those graveyards, the visitors' book of a house in the country, and found this book of Friday's Hill, where I generally spent my summers, full, as such books always are, of the names of persons who have died, or at least have faded from one's life.

In addition to our guests, other of our friends and acquaintances would rent cottages for the summer, or take lodgings for a month or two in the neighborhood. I remember the Michael Fields thus settled, and the Alfred Whiteheads, and one year a large black contingent of Steins would darken our drive, led by the great Gertrude herself.

All these would settle like a flock of birds on our terrace, where tea was provided and the talk was free. This talk must have sounded extremely silly to my mother when that amused old lady sat writing her religious books at a table just inside the open window.

[223]

We were many of us authors, but my mother was, I think, the only one of us whose books would sell, and they would sell in thousands. Occasionally she would receive what we thought meagre checks from her publishers; but when we suggested that she should ask for better terms, she showed (what she seldom showed) a certain annoyance with us.

"My publishers," she would say, "are deeply religious men; they write me the most beautiful Christian letters, and I am sure they send me for my books all they can conveniently afford. I don't write my books for money, and I don't like thinking or talking of money in connection with them."

The crowning glory of these Fernhurst seasons was the reception given once a year by the wife of the village doctor. Those of us who were invited would sit on uncomfortable chairs in the little garden of her red brick villa, and talk of the aristocracy. The imagination of our hostess shed such an air of grandeur over these assemblies that, though I have had occasional glimpses since then of what the world calls greatness, all of them have seemed in comparison somehow shabby and second-rate, and not quite the thing.

With the autumn all these glories would fade away, and I would return to the solitude of High Buildings.

"*O solitudo, sola beatitudo*," Santayana quotes from Saint Bernard, adding that this saint of a great mind and a great heart had accepted as true the verdict which antiquity had passed, after a long and brilliant experience of it, on society — that it was essentially a moral failure. Saint Bernard had meant, Santayana explained, that happiness lies, not in absolute solitude, but in the substitution of an ideal for a natural society, in converse with thoughts rather than with things. Such a substitution, he adds, is normal, and a mark of moral vigor.

"To substitute the society of ideas for that of things is," he says, "simply to live in the mind; it is to survey the world of existences

in its truth and beauty rather than in its
personal perspectives, or with practical ur-
gency. It is the sole path of happiness for
the intellectual man, because the intellectual
man cannot be satisfied with a world of per-
petual change, defeat, and imperfection."
The world, he adds, regards this way of living
as rather ghostly and poor. But the solitary
"usually congratulates himself upon it at the
end; and of those who persevere some become
saints and some poets and some philosophers."

I cannot pretend that this sublime doctrine
of solitude was what led me to live alone at
High Buildings. But it was a cheap way of
living, and the word *Loneliness*, which Henry
James said I must inscribe on my banner,
had not, and has never had, any terrors for
me. I liked living by myself; some of my happiest moments had come to me in solitude,
and what unlimited hours had been mine for
reading! Besides, according to my notion, the
youth of every generation paints the same
picture or writes much the same kind of prose

or poetry. Then little by little, or sometimes suddenly, those few who are fated to do so find their originality, their special note or vision — their "virtue," as we say of a herb or jewel, the thing that they, and they alone, can do. A secret door seems to open for them into a realm of imagination which is theirs alone.

Such things don't happen to prophets seated in their family circles, or to poets in society. Prophets retire to the desert to meditate their message, and it is generally to poets when they are alone that these secret doors open. Certainly, in the social life I had led in Paris, nothing of the kind had happened to me. Given an American who had been at Oxford, and who wanted to write a book about it, might it not have been foretold that he would write a book very much like the one I had written? But making the assumption, which was very unlikely, yet natural enough for me to make, that I was something more than a mere product of the ideas and influences of my time, might it not

be possible that in a long spell of solitude
something might come to the top that was
authentically my own? So I settled down to
continue practising the art of writing; and
with Pater still as my model. In many ways I
could not have chosen a worse one. Pater had
elaborated for himself a style suited to ren-
der his own somewhat remote and sophisti-
cated sense of life; but the more appropriate
it was for the expression of his own sensi-
bility, the more inappropriate and insincere
it became in the hands of others. It was
moreover also extremely imitable; but the
delicate music of his phrasing became, in
those who copied him, a kind of melancholy
bleat — a cooing, as of lugubrious doves
moaning under depressing circumstances a
muffled kind of monotonous singsong. "The
yellowing leaves of the lime trees, the creeper
that flushed to so deep a crimson against the
old grey walls, the chrysanthemums that shed
so prodigally their petals on the smooth green
lawn — all these things, beautiful and wonderful as they were, were somehow a little

melancholy also, as being signs of the year's decay." Thus Max Beerbohm parodies the prose of one of Pater's imitators.

I have just been reading with some amusement, mingled with a touch of pathos, four volumes of a journal in which, during this period, I noted down my moods and impressions. It is a curious record, the record of an attempt to see things elegantly and nobly in the Paterian spirit, and to find for each chosen impression its perfect and melodious phrase. These old journals are almost intolerable reading, for their author was not after all any more than Pater himself, an Imaginary Portrait, and their pages are tainted with sentimentality, insincerity, and pose. And yet at moments, as I read, the memory of that lost mood has for me a certain beauty. I seem to hear the sound, as it were, of church bells in the distance recalling me to that long Sabbath of the soul. I don't regret this infatuation which held me under its enchantment so long. It was the happiest period of my life; and are not the joys of vanity delicious? What

mortal is happier after all than the compla-
cent, self-satisfied, self-applauding prig?

But seriously I do not think I could have
spent these years in a more profitable fashion.
I was free at any rate from cheap aims and
mean ambitions; I did not associate with
second-rate or dull people; I loved reading,
I was still only half-educated, and there is a
kind of charm, a dreamlike quality of life,
which grows as one spends one day after
another by oneself. That I found in my solitude anything original to write, that a door
opened for me into a realm of my own, would
be too much to claim; but along with Pater's
volumes I had with me a volume of Baudelaire's, which I read with equal enthusiasm
and, I like to think, with more profit. What
writer, he asked in this little volume of Prose
Poems, has not, in his moments of ambition,
dreamt of a prose, musical without rhythm
or rhyme, supple and abrupt enough to express the sudden joys of the spirit, the undu-
lations of our reveries, the ups and downs of
our moods? Such a book of prose might be

composed, like a book of verses, of loosely connected or disconnected fragments; they could be cut in pieces, but each piece would have a life of its own, and some of them life enough to amuse the reader.

Studying this little book, it occurred to me that the separate page or paragraph of prose had not been adequately exploited. Every aspect of existence I believed could find its best expression in some special literary form. But in the experience of each of us were there not moods, brief impressions, and modern ways of feeling for which no exactly appropriate way of expression was at hand?

This was the notion that began to haunt me in odd moments. Something like Baudelaire in style was what I dreamed of; but a style more idiomatic, more colloquial, yet capable of rising to the heights of poetic English prose. But what was it exactly that wanted to find expression in the little book I meditated? They were not things that lay on the surface of consciousness, ready to be put into words. The world is full of conscious

[231]

thoughts, which have found adequate expression; but I was haunted now and then by intimations which seemed to have a significance which I could not understand. The things that seemed to want to be said were latent meanings which no one had yet put into words; which would have to find the words themselves for their expression. In a sentence overheard in conversation, or in something which, often to my surprise, I would hear myself saying, or in the memory of an exaltation or humiliation or grotesque encounter, there would seem to lie a meaning, an ironic, grotesque, perhaps a profound significance. I became more and more haunted by a sense of the oddity of existence, of the fact that, as Plato hinted, this universe is not one which should be taken too seriously, or that our personal affairs were not worthy of the care and anxiety that the ignominy of our existence forced us to bestow upon them.

"No, no!" my subconscious mind would peevishly exclaim, when I tried to write down one of these odd bits of reverie or meditation or of wanton thought. "No! That is n't in the least what I want to say!" So I would try again and yet again; and once in a while the voice would grudgingly remark, "Well, yes, I think that that will have to do."

At last I inserted a few of these experiments in a pretentious little review which the Berensons and I printed privately at Fiesole in 1897. We called it the *Golden Urn*. It contained also a list of the best, and only the best, Italian pictures in galleries and private collections, and anthologies of what we thought the finest lines in Shakespeare, Milton, and Keats.

I have always been fond of anthologizing. I think it a dainty occupation for a person of leisure and literary tastes. I have published several of these volumes; but the anthology in which I took the greatest pride is my *Little Essays from the Writings of George Santayana*, since the works of that wise and beautiful writer were at that time almost unknown to the English public.

In 1902 I felt that my own book of prose was polished to a point beyond which I could not make it better. No publisher would of course accept so odd a book, but I printed it in a small edition, and perhaps thirty copies were sold. It was regarded, I think, as a discreditable failure, especially by my Cambridge friends.

From Oxford came a gleam of appreciation, for Robert Bridges wrote me a set of verses in which, though he felt he must express his disapproval of the idle life I seemed to be living, he could not help praising the "hallowed leisure, the music and peace of the soul," which that way of living seemed to provide.

It was not till sixteen years later that I found to my astonishment that this little book was not altogether dead. My friend Desmond MacCarthy drew one day a copy from his pocket and told me that he often read from it to certain people who seemed to like it, and he asked me for more of the same kind of thing to print in the *New Statesman*, of which he was then the literary editor. I was of course delighted to comply with his request, and finally in 1918 all this material was made into a book, for which I borrowed from Gay the title of *Trivia*. It was published and it sold, and has gone on steadily selling ever since. Translations of it were made into several foreign languages, and the book has had a larger circulation, I believe, in France than in England. This circumstance has an inclination to make me feel that across the Channel there is more appreciation than on this side of originality in writing.

Among the letters about the book which have been sent me, I highly prize an indignant one from a Mormon in Salt Lake City, who demanded by what right I had presumed to put into print his private thoughts and feelings. And now that I have begun boasting (and surely there is nothing pleasanter in the world than boasting), I shall permit myself to quote a letter, not from Salt Lake City, but from Rome, in which George Santayana writes of *Trivia*: "The whole makes a picture of the self-consciousness of the modern man which is not only delightfully vivid and humorous, but a document of importance as well. For although it represents only one side of yourself or of any of us, it is just the side which the age has made conspicuous. Men have always been the victims of trifles, but when they were uncomfortable, and passionate, and in constant danger, they hardly had time to notice what the daily texture of their thoughts was in their calm intervals; whereas with us the intervals are all, and that is what you have painted."

He found it delightful, he said, to live in a world such as I had painted, full of pictures and incidental *divertissements* and amiable absurdities. When Robert Bridges said to him that I had written the most immoral book in the world, though every word could be read in any drawing-room, he had replied that the book was not in his opinion at all immoral; it was meant to be light and irresponsible, not complete and ultimate. "And why," he asked, "should not things be largely absurd, futile, and transitory? They are so, and we are so, and we and they go very well together."

Santayana felt it incumbent on him, however, to reprove me for a technical heresy touching the separation of the soul and the body, which he said neither he nor Aristotle would admit, in this world any more than in the other. This heresy involves of course the doctrine of the Resurrection of the Body — that fundamental teaching of the Christian faith. I had already received a letter from an aged and opulent aunt in America, reproving me sharply for the same heretical opinion. I have never yet discovered on which page of *Trivia* Santayana and my maiden aunt detected this error, but I have always believed that it cost me a fortune, as my aunt, who had regarded me, I had always thought, as her favorite nephew, bequeathed the wealth I had expected from her to another heir.

But this is enough, or too much, about the costly little book born in the solitude of the Sussex woods.

9

Hunting for Manuscripts

ENGLAND has become the home of sport for many Americans, who come annually to this island for deer stalking, for fishing, and for the hunting of foxes. But there is another form of hunting which has occupied a good deal of my English leisure — the hunting, namely, for manuscripts of literary interest in English archives and old English country houses. I acquired my taste for this form of sport when I began to write the life of the old poet and ambassador and Provost of Eton, Sir Henry Wotton; and I spent some years in collecting his unpublished letters. The archives of the Record Office, the British Museum, and the Bodleian

Library are easily accessible, and there are officials at these institutions ready and even eager to assist students in their labors. But I soon became aware that distinguished biographers preferred to make use of printed sources rather than to pursue their researches among unpublished papers. I found that since Walton's biography at least seven sketches, portraits, and lives of Wotton had been written by scholars of distinction, including Adolphus Ward and Sir Sidney Lee, but that none of these had looked at his dispatches, of which at least five hundred were preserved unread in the Record Office, or at his letters to be found in the British Museum. All these were, of course, easily accessible; one had only to ask for the packet which might contain a document of interest, and the packet would be brought to one's reading desk by a polite official.

When, however, I wished to pursue my hunting into the archives of private houses, I found that a much more elaborate method of procedure was required. It is quite useless, in my experience, to write out of the blue, so to speak, to great personages and ask permission to examine their muniments rooms and inherited manuscripts. Either they will not reply, or they will send curt refusals. I think that they do not know themselves (not being literate people) what treasures they possess; or if they do, they regard an unknown inquirer as a thief or gangster, with robbery as the object of his visit. I found it necessary, therefore, to procure some kind of personal introduction before writing to them. The plan I adopted was that of inquiring among the people I happened to meet if any of them knew, or knew anything about, the magnate whose manuscripts I wanted to examine; and once a personal relation of this kind was formed, however tenuous, all difficulties would at once vanish.

The world allots but meagre rewards to researchers; it allows them in recompense, however, the privilege of describing the discoveries they have made, and thus of enjoying what is one of the least reprehensible forms of human vanity — a form of self-glory not very amiably denominated by the inglorious term of "boasting." Undeterred, however, by that epithet, I shall avail myself of the scholar's license — a license also shared by anglers — by mentioning a few of my successes in this special sport.

In examining the Seventh Report of the Historical Manuscripts Commission, I found a note by A. J. Horwood, who had been sent in 1878 to examine the manuscripts at a great mansion near Oakham, of a manuscript volume which contained "copies of letters seemingly by and to Sir Henry Wotton." I found that this house was in the possession of a certain elderly colonel, and I began inquiring among the people I met if any of them knew him. At last I met an old lady who was his cousin, and who kindly said that I might write to him and make use of her name as an introduction. I therefore wrote, and received a most courteous answer from the colonel, saying that he knew nothing of the manuscript book, and did not believe he possessed it, but that he was quite willing for me to come and look for it myself.

I thereupon went to Oakham, and took a cab up to an immense Italian villa, which is one of the biggest houses in England, if not the biggest. I drove into a great colonnaded courtyard of about twenty acres (larger, I believe, than the Great Court of Trinity College, Cambridge), and up to the splendid steps of the mansion — steps partially broken and partially overgrown with weeds, for the whole place looked ill-kept and considerably out of repair, as if funds were not abundant on that hilltop. I rang the great resounding front-door bell, and the stately portal was opened by an old gentleman in a shawl, who reminded me of the Duke of Wellington in his appearance. I introduced myself, and mentioned his cousin, of whom we talked awhile, and then I stated my errand, at which he gave a somewhat malicious chuckle and showed me into an immense library, which occupied one wing of the great house and looked about a mile long. It was full of débris, pictures without frames, frames without pictures, old rocking-horses without heads, and was lined with immense old bookshelves, reaching to ceilings that seemed to touch the sky. "Now you can have a look, and you must let me give you luncheon later," he said, and then he disappeared.

It was a cold day in November; the library was unheated, and I felt the beginnings of a violent cold upon me. My despair at the gigantic search in prospect (which would have required weeks at least for its satisfactory performance) can be imagined; but still I felt that, having come so far, I must take at least a look. While I was doing this, I happened to see the colonel with two maiden ladies (whom I afterwards found to be his daughters) staring at me through an immense window from the terrace outside. By great good fortune I found within half an hour the book I was looking for, and saw at once that it was of even greater interest than I had hoped, as it contained copies of many of Wotton's unpublished letters, a number of documents concerning his first embassy at Venice (1604–1610), and a large collection of notes of "table talk," kept by someone in his household at Venice during that period, with many anecdotes about Queen Elizabeth, James I, Henry IV, Bacon and Essex, and various personages of the time, as well as a number of poems by Donne and others, a copy of Donne's *Paradoxes*, with a long unpublished letter which Donne sent with them, and a number of other early, unpublished letters by Donne, some signed and some unsigned, all of which had escaped Horwood's notice when he examined the manuscript.

I took the book to the colonel's study, where there was a good fire, and where the old gentleman sat reading *The Times*. Occasionally I caught his eye, staring at me over its pages as if he were asking himself what sort of creature I could be to take so great an interest in old papers.

When at last I hinted that it would take me more than an afternoon to master and copy out the contents of this volume, he most kindly asked me to come and pay him a visit for this purpose. I was, of course, delighted to accept this invitation, and spent several days in this great seventeenth-century palace, whose wide terraces overlooked perhaps the most famous of English hunting countries. I had my meals with the colonel and his daughters, and attended divine service with them in the chapel of the house. They all treated me with the perfect courtesy of their class, and made no attempt to find out who I was, or what motive had induced me to engage in this (to them) so incomprehensible a form of sport. They were much too polite to ask any questions.

When I found that the period of my visit was insufficient for an adequate study of the contents of this book, I arranged for the Oxford Press to purchase its copyright, and to have the volume sent to Oxford for careful copies to be made. Sir Herbert Grierson came to Oxford to examine the poems, which he afterwards published in his masterly edition of Donne's poems. I remember that when he and I were shut up together to examine this volume in a big room at the top of the Clarendon Press, Satan tempted me to make the suggestion that it would be rather fun to insert among these perfectly unknown notes of table talk some chance remark about Bacon as a playwright which might set the Baconians agog; and I remember Grierson's expression of horror at this suggestion, which it is indeed lucky we did n't carry out, since, shortly after the volume was returned to the place where I had found it, the house was burnt down and the manuscript destroyed.

I published the letters of Wotton and the table talk (with which, I need hardly say, I did not tamper) in my Life of Wotton. The letters of Donne (which were of great interest) were published by Mrs. Simpson in her *Study of the Prose Works of John Donne*, and reprinted by John Hayward in the Nonesuch Donne.

Some years later, when Mrs. Toynbee was editing Horace Walpole's letters, and I happened to be specially interested in Walpole at the time, I wrote to her (although I did not know her) saying that I hoped she would print more of Walpole's letters to Madame du Deffand, since the extracts from them published by Miss Berry seemed to me of such interest and merit. She replied that she would gladly do so, but that the box containing the Walpole-du-Deffand correspondence had not been traced since its sale at Strawberry Hill in 1842, and that no one knew where it was. Encouraged, I suppose, by a series of other successes in hunting for manuscripts in country houses, I replied with a rashness which now seems to me preposterous that I would find that box for her if she would tell me all she knew about it. She replied that it was supposed to have been bought at Strawberry Hill by a man of Asiatic origin named Dyce-Sombre, and that nothing had been heard of it since.

I looked up the history of the purchaser of this box, and found that it was an extraordinary one. His great-grandfather was a German carpenter, who went to India in 1754, and, becoming a soldier in the service of several native princes, acquired the appellation of Sombre — from his serious cast of countenance — instead of his German name Reinhard, and was given by the emperor of Delhi the principality of Sirdhama. This passed on his death to his wife, a dancing girl, who became the Begum of that state. Sombre in the meantime had begotten by a concubine a son called Zuffer yah Khan. Zuffer Khan died, leaving a daughter, who married George Alexander Dyce, the commandant of the Begum's forces. The son by this marriage inherited half a million sterling from the Begum at her decease, and added the name of Sombre to that of Dyce. He became a Roman Catholic, and was created by the Pope a chevalier of the Order of Christ, in consideration of the very large gifts the Begum had made to His Holiness.

In 1838, Dyce-Sombre came to England, where he married the daughter of an English peer. He entered Parliament and then a lunatic asylum, and died in 1851; and his wife, from whom he had been long separated, married a man of fortune who was afterwards created a peer under the title of Lord F. His title and estate were inherited by his son.

It was with this Begum's money that the desired box had been purchased; and I had a feeling, what is called a "hunch," that the box was now in the possession, and reposed in the country house, of Lord F.

I cannot account for this hunch, but it amounted to so strong a conviction that I began again my tedious process of trying to establish some sort of relation with this backwoods peer, who lived in Staffordshire, and of whom no one I met seemed to have ever heard. At last I met in Florence a young man who told me that this Lord F. was the intimate friend of his cousin, the Dean of York, and suggested that I should write to the Dean, saying that he had told me I might do so. This suggestion I adopted; and after making inquiries as to how a letter to a Dean should be properly addressed, I sent a polite epistle to the Very Reverend gentleman (who

I found was himself a man of letters, having written a book on *The Heraldry of York Minster*). I received a most courteous reply from the Dean, who said yes, Lord F. was his friend, and that I had better write to him, telling him that he (the Dean) had told me to do so. I thereupon wrote to Lord F., delicately suggesting that the Dean of York was a great pal of mine, and asking him if he happened to possess among his archives this box from Strawberry Hill.

Thereupon I waited for some weeks, perhaps a month or two, but received no answer. Then came a letter from Mrs. Toynbee, reminding me that I had agreed to find these letters, and telling me that she was holding up her edition of Walpole for them; and well, so to speak, what about it? I sat down and wrote a letter of apology to the irritated lady, saying that I had been far too presumptuous in making this promise, in which I regretted to say that I had completely failed.

I was living at High Buildings at the time, and used to walk to the village post office every day to get my letters. Before dropping my letter to Mrs. Toynbee in the box, I opened one addressed to me, which turned out to be from Lord F. himself, in which he wrote, with many apologies, to say that he had mislaid my note and had only come on it that morning; whereupon he had gone up to his attic and had found there the box about which I had written, and which he had had no notion that he possessed. It would be, he feared, of no interest to me, as he had found, on examining the letters in it, that some autograph collector had cut off the signatures from them. However, he politely added, if I cared to come to Staffordshire he would put the box at my disposal, to make any use I wished of its contents. He ended with messages of regard to our common friend, the Dean of York. I tore up my first letter, therefore, to Mrs. Toynbee, and went home to write another to her, in which I said that, having promised to find this box, I had, of course, done so, and that it was now in Lord F.'s attic in Staffordshire, and if she would write

[252]

to him, mentioning my name and that of the Dean of York, he would no doubt put it at her disposal.

Thereupon Mrs. Toynbee (with, I think, her husband, Paget Toynbee) went leaping up to Staffordshire, and found that the box contained even greater treasures than she could have hoped for — hundreds and hundreds of unpublished letters from Madame du Deffand, who was only second in fame as a letter writer to Madame de Sévigné. They were all annotated (evidently for publication) by Horace Walpole himself, and among them were a certain number of Walpole's own letters, though he seems to have destroyed most of these on account of the bad French in which he believed that they had been written. Mrs. Toynbee spent some years in preparing a scholarly edition of these manuscripts, and this edition was published in three big volumes, after her death, by her husband.

I confess that my angler's vanity was a little hurt by the fact that no copy of this book was sent to me, and that my share in this catch was not referred to. This, however, may have been due to the fact that Mrs. Toynbee was dead when her husband brought out the book.

My last experience of this sport I should like to put on record — not that I have any grievance to air, but because I think it may prove one day of interest to literary historians. I happened to see last year in David Alec Wilson's portentous life of Carlyle a statement that Carlyle's letters to the second Lord Ashburton were in the possession of a certain noble marquis, now deceased. Again that voice told me that his son had somewhere in his possession the whole Carlyle-Ashburton correspondence. So I began trying to find someone who was acquainted with him; and at last a lady who was a friend of mine told me that she knew him and his wife very well, and promised to ask them when she next saw them whether they had these letters. Not long after she wrote to say that she had inquired, and that they said they did n't have them and knew nothing about them. I replied that I thought her noble friends might do well to have another look, as one letter at least had been seen not long ago by Carlyle's biographer. Shortly afterwards I received a note which I first thought was the rudest, and then saw was one of the kindest, I had ever received from one of these noble but unlettered personages who so curiously combine incivility to strangers with generosity and courtesy to anyone who may seem to have some connection with anyone of their class.

The letter was addressed to "Mr. (or Mrs.) L. P. Smith," and, beginning "Dear Sir or Madam," stated that the writer had received two scrawls from my friend, neither of which he could read, and so thought it better to write to me direct. He had, he said, the Carlyle letters, but they were of a distinctly personal nature, being addressed to members of his family now deceased. He had looked at them, but could not see that they possessed any interest; however, he would be delighted to lend me typewritten copies of them, if I would undertake to submit to him any extracts from them before I made use of them for publication.

I of course answered that I should be very glad to see these copies, and I offered to pay to have them made. No notice was taken of this offer; and in a few months I received a heap of typewritten copies of the Carlyle correspondence — 256 letters of Carlyle's, 27 of Mrs. Carlyle's, and other documents concerning the relations of the Carlyles and the Ashburtons, all of them unpublished. Of Carlyle's letters 121 were to the first Lady Ashburton (Lady Harriet Baring), 94 to the second, and 41 to Lord Ashburton, the whole correspondence covering a period of thirty-four years.

I found them very interesting reading — Carlyle being to my mind one of the best of letter writers, and Mrs. Carlyle, of course, always fascinating. Carlyle was at his best in writing to the Barings. The letters to Lady Harriet show that he was considerably be-

witched by this great lady, and that Mrs.
Carlyle had some reason to be jealous. Her
successor, Louisa, Lady Ashburton, was of a
very different character, and proved herself
to be the good angel of Carlyle, and also of
Mrs. Carlyle, with whom she formed a most
devoted friendship. She too was a clever
woman, who, after the death of her husband,
became engaged to Robert Browning. But
she broke off the engagement, to his great
indignation, and he is supposed to have written the famous lines to her: —

> Would it were I had been false, not you!
>   I that am nothing, not you that are all:
> I, never the worse for a touch or two
>   On my speckled hide —

The owner of these letters wrote me that
I could take extracts from them, but that he
would reserve the right of refusing, even at
the last moment, to allow any extract to be
printed. The whole correspondence he would
not permit to be published, as he did n't want
to have anyone making money out of the
friendships of his relations. I did not feel like

undertaking any publication under the supervision of this kind, but arbitrary and unlettered, nobleman. I therefore returned them to him, with due thanks for letting me see them, and they are still in his possession. I feel that a book ought sometime to be made of them, since the friendship of the Carlyles with the Ashburtons was the most important friendship of their lives, and in writing to all three of them both the Carlyles wrote their best. Through friends and relations of the owner of these manuscripts I have made several attempts to obtain permission for such a volume to be edited and published by some competent person, but so far my efforts have been in vain. But one day no doubt these letters will see the light. They will make a volume full of good reading and of important literary interest.

Only the other day I had a queer experience, and thought for a moment that I had heard that plaguy voice again. I was sitting at luncheon by a lady who is a scholar of repute, and, speaking of manuscripts, she told me that her first job was to catalogue the manuscripts and books at Gorhambury for the Lord Verulam of the time. She said that in poking about, somewhat indiscreetly, in an old cupboard, she had found, under a heap of rubbish, a number of old playbills of Shakespeare's plays. She found that in fact her search had been an indiscretion; Lord Verulam did not want anything to be known about these playbills, as he had been much bothered by Baconian cranks and did not care to have them after him again.

Playbills of Shakespeare's age are, I believe, unknown, and that bills of some of Shakespeare's plays should be found in the home of Bacon's heir seemed to me a suggestion full of disagreeable possibilities, but one which perhaps it was my duty as a scholar to follow up. On writing, however, to the lady in question, I received the following reassuring reply.

Yes, I really did say we found Shakespearean playbills at Gorhambury in 1911 or thereabouts

— but while old they were far from being contemporary. They would be waste of a scholar's time — if they still exist — but would in those days have provided a lot of healthy exercise for a Baconian Heretic.

In this sport of hunting for manuscripts in English country houses, either I have had extraordinary luck, or else such houses are full of treasures for those who will take the trouble to hunt for them. But it is necessary to acquire the technique of pursuing this form of chase — a form, to my mind, superior in interest to that of fishing for big fish or of hunting foxes. And there are not only letters to reward the hunters. In the last year or two a manuscript of the first literary importance has been discovered in an old country house, *The Book of Marjorie Kempe*, a frank autobiography written in the most vivid and enchanting style, and full of incredible avowals. It is by centuries the earliest autobiography in English, and indeed a great open window into the life of the early fifteenth century.

Commonplace books full of contemporary verse abound also in old libraries, which have never been examined by persons with a taste for poetry of merit. Many Elizabethans wrote beautiful poems which they never thought of printing, but circulated among their friends, who made copies of them. I have already mentioned the beautiful unpublished verses in the volume of Wotton's letters which I found, some of which have appeared in recent anthologies. The only other volume I know of which has been examined from the point of view of literary merit is the volume, now famous, in the Christ Church library, in which poems were found of surpassing beauty that have become permanent additions to our treasure of Elizabethan poetry.

10

The Expatriates

T HE CRUISE on the Ægean, during which I have worked almost every morning in writing my reminiscences, is almost over; after visiting Cyprus, Crete, and Egypt, we have crossed the Mediterranean and reach this afternoon the harbor of Hyères, where we take leave of each other. We have spent ten weeks of perfect weather in perfect accord; and I don't remember more than one serious dispute among us. The subject of this argument was that of peonies. Edith Wharton, our hostess, declared that the peony was a plant indigenous to the East; it had been introduced into Europe, she affirmed, from China and Japan. I said the plant was native to Europe also, where it grew wild in various regions. My opponent knew a great deal more about plants and gardens than I did, but on this point it happened that I was right. I think she would have liked to have beaten me till I was black and blue, as my mother had done when she attempted to beat the Old Adam out of me as a baby. But again, as in that early encounter, I did not yield an inch. She grew still more exasperated when I quoted at her Spratt's *Travels and Researches in Crete*, which we happened to have on board, and in which the author speaks of the wild peonies he had found on that island. She expressed the greatest contempt for Spratt; Spratt could n't, as his book proved, see what was before his eyes, and would certainly not have known a peony if he had come into a wilderness of them. Mrs. Winthrop Chanler and the two other members of our party gazed at the view and wisely said nothing.

Edith Wharton was an extraordinarily shy person; meeting strangers frightened her, and to protect herself against them she would assume the air and manner of the aristocratic

New Yorker she had happened to be born. This assumption of a great lady's manner was unfortunate, as it tended to terrify the people of whom she herself stood in terror. But at a gleam of sympathy and consideration there would emerge, as from some prickly carapace, one of the most intelligent, witty, and freest of human beings I have ever known, and one of the most tender and loyal of friends. She loved good conversation and ribaldry and laughter, and with her, as with Walt Whitman, one could sit and talk with the wildest freedom all day, and on every subject — except perhaps the original habitat of peonies.

It may be of interest to recall my first meeting with her. I was staying a good many years ago with the Berensons near Florence. B.B., as we all called him, who had been present thirty years earlier at that lecture of Gosse's which I have described, had now achieved a European reputation as an authority on the painters of Italy, and Botticelli among them. He had married my elder sister after the death of her first husband, and it so

happened that we were all three invited to
luncheon at a neighboring villa to meet Mrs.
Wharton. We gladly accepted the invitation,
expecting to derive much pleasure from making the acquaintance of a cultivated and
clever woman of whom we had heard a great
deal. Disconcerting, however, was our experience when we found ourselves treated by
this American writer with what seemed a
mingling of intellectual and social contempt.
Berenson, accustomed as he was to much consideration, even deference, grew more and
more indignant. My sister did n't like it
either, and to tell the truth, I by no means
found it pleasant to be rolled, as we all felt
we were rolled, in the mud on this occasion.

We drove away full of indignation, and
Berenson, who took things much more hardly
than my sister and myself, resolved never
again to meet Mrs. Wharton. When, some
months later, he was in Paris, he would accept
no invitation without stipulating that he
should not find himself in her company. This
caused much amusement, but more incon-

venience in the cosmopolitan society which
they both frequented; and finally Henry
Adams, who was a friend equally of the
Berensons and Mrs. Wharton, arranged a
tea party in which the company sat in the
semi-darkness of firelight. Berenson found
himself in conversation with a voice beside
him (the speaker he could not see); and the
wit and sensitiveness of his unseen neighbor,
the freedom of her spirit, her reading, and her
sense of fun, made him, as the phrase now is,
fall for her in the completest sense of this
modern term. Then the lights were turned
on and he saw that his interlocutor was Edith
Wharton, whom he hated. But, alas! it was
now too late; they were united as by a hoop
of steel in a friendship that endured till Mrs.
Wharton's death.

She often visited the Berensons and they
loved to stay with her. They all three became
companions and in every way the best of
friends. When they once discussed their first
disastrous meeting Mrs. Wharton would not
admit her haughtiness towards us; of this fail-

ing she was absolutely unconscious, but the cause of it, her terror at the thought of meeting the Berensons, and her shyness when she met them, she vividly described.

I have said that nothing shocked Edith Wharton, but to this statement one qualification must be made. Her worldly carapace was not completely detachable; there were breaches of Knickerbocker etiquette which she did n't like at all. If, as I am afraid sometimes happened, I carelessly sat down on her right at the luncheon table when some older or more distinguished man was present, she was definitely put out. Again, to be referred to in the press as "Mrs. Edith Wharton" annoyed her very much. The use of "Mrs." before the Christian name of a married woman is something which, for some reason I fail to understand, makes people of social position shudder; and unluckily this solecism would not infrequently occur in the columns of that review which Mrs. Wharton read with special interest, the Literary Supplement of *The Times*. Knowing how much it annoyed her, I finally protested to the editor of this publication, who was a friend of mine. He replied to my letter with many apologies; it was a pure mischance; the last instance had occurred when he was away; it should certainly not occur again. But it did recur; there was a fatality about it, and editors fight against compositors in vain.

But there was another matter to me of much graver consequence, concerning which I did try to save Mrs. Wharton from ignominy, though fruitlessly once more. Of etiquette on land I possess no special knowledge, but to me, as a yachtsman, the stately snobbery of the sea is not a laughing matter. I cannot regard burgees with indifference, or mock at the membership of yachting clubs they imply. I find that marine splendors are exempt from the great law proclaimed by the Bible, that all is vanity beneath the sun. To sail into a harbor full of yachts under the burgee of the Royal Yacht Squadron, and in a boat flying the white ensign of the Royal Navy, — a

[269]

privilege granted alone to that most exclusive of all the clubs of this universe, — to gaze with contempt at all the other vessels, even from another person's yacht, is a glory which I feel no saint, however heavenly-minded, could decently despise.

When I embarked as Mrs. Wharton's guest on the great white yacht she had chartered from England for our Mediterranean cruise, I told her that she, as charterer of the yacht, would have difficulties to cope with which she must face both with courage and with knowledge of yachting etiquette. She had hired the yacht with skipper, crew, and cook complete, and it was for her to pay all their wages, as well as tip them generously when the cruise was over. To treat them, therefore, merely as her hired servants, paid to carry out her orders, would be, unless she was extremely careful, to bring disgrace upon herself and on us all. To seamen the land-lubber is an object of infinite contempt; to treat him with every courtesy, and at the same time to make him into a laughingstock

among the knowing, is their legitimate delight. By this sentiment, I told her, the skipper of the *Osprey* would certainly be ani-
mated, and he would also desire to carry on
the cruise to his own convenience and take
things as easy as he could. He knew himself
to be a person of great importance, empow-
ered by law to put us all, if necessary, in irons;
and between such a potentate and the de-
spised, landlubbery American lady from
whom he deigned to take his wages, a conflict
was certain to arise. If she wished the cruise
to be hers, rather than the skipper's, it was of
the highest importance to gain the upper
hand in their first encounter. She must not,
however, allow the clash of wills to occur on
some technical point — the exact course to
be pursued, the place to anchor, or the
weather in which to set sail again. On all
such technical points, her knowledge could
not cope with his, and she would certainly be
defeated. "Choose, therefore," I advised her,
"some point of mere convenience, where
nothing but your own comfort is concerned.

There is, for instance," I added, "a smart motor launch in the davits, in which we ought to dash ashore with our ensign flying, and amid the admiration of all beholders. But to lower this launch is a bother, while the rowing boat is always ready. To save himself and his men trouble, the skipper will want to have us rowed ashore. But if you say firmly, 'Skipper, we will have the launch,' he will be obliged to obey your orders."

This crisis soon arose. Mrs. Wharton, accustomed to unquestioned obedience from butler, footmen, gardeners, and chauffeurs on land, lost her spirit on the terrifying sea. The words I had suggested trembled on her lips, but they trembled there unspoken; the launch remained in the davits, and we were rowed ashore. I knew at once that the cruise was to be the skipper's cruise, not Mrs. Wharton's. Being a man of kindly nature, and hoping, moreover, for a handsome tip when our voyage was over, the skipper was always willing to consider her wishes, but they were to him no more than wishes; he never put out to sea but when the weather was to his liking; being a strict Presbyterian from Paisley, he always stopped our voyage, wherever we might be, to enable himself and the crew to observe the strictest Scottish Sabbath; and he would always anchor, as skippers love to anchor, as far as possible from the shore. Thither we would be conveyed in a rowing boat. Sometimes, indeed, he would forget even to send a rowing boat to fetch us back on board, and we would be forced to hire a local boat for our return.

The disgrace of going aboard or leaving a yacht or vessel of the navy in a boat hired from the shore is not understood by people who do not frequent the sea. I remember once discussing with a naval man the famous *Dreadnaught* incident, when a party of intellectuals from Bloomsbury, including Virginia Woolf, dressed themselves up as Abyssinian princes and paid a state visit to the *Dreadnaught*, inflicting thereby in nautical opinion an insult on the British navy which many thought should be punished by legal action.

What would have happened, I asked my naval acquaintance, if, while the party were being officially received aboard the *Dreadnaught*, it had been discovered that they were frauds, and that one of the supposed princes was a woman? He looked at me gravely, and replied that they would have been sent off the *Dreadnaught* in a shore boat, thereby incurring a degradation of which not one of the party would have been in the least aware.

In omitting to send even a rowing boat to take us to the yacht, the skipper, while providing joy to the little port where we were anchored, inflicted a slight on Mrs. Wharton of which he knew she would never have an inkling. To see this stately lady, conscious from birth of her dignity and position, and a little over-anxious, in my opinion, to assert them, placed in a position from which all dignity was absent was a hardship which I was capable of bearing. A slight touch of friendly malice and amusement towards those we love keeps our affection for them, I find, from becoming flat.

But I must put an end to my reflections and pack up my books and papers, since we leave the *Osprey* in a few hours. On this occasion I hope we shall be allowed the motor launch for our departure.

We were allowed the launch when we landed about ten years ago. And now our hostess, who treated us with such kindness, and whom we loved, and loved all the more for her little weaknesses, has gone her ways, and I must follow soon. We are indeed leaves that perish, as Homer told us long ago. I do not find that a fate to be regretted; to ask for a greater length of years would be to solicit the almost certainty of many miseries; and for any other form of being I feel no longing. All that I have read about what happens in a future existence makes the life beyond the grave seem an uncomfortable adventure. I have no desire for eternal bliss. And in the meantime I am able to enjoy, and I much enjoy, what Walt Whitman described as "old age flowing free, with the delicious near-by assurance of Death."

The record of my youth and boyhood which I took ashore with me from the *Osprey* I more or less forgot. One evening, however, years afterwards, when staying with my sister, Mrs. Berenson, at Florence, I fished it out and read aloud to the company some of the pages, which they liked. It was suggested that I should send them to the *Atlantic Monthly*, which Mr. Berenson, who reads everything, declared to be, with the *Revue des Deux Mondes*, one of the two best reviews which are now published. This suggestion lingered in my mind; and finally, on what occasion I have forgotten, or for what reason, I did send them to Boston. The editor of the *Atlantic* printed them, but asked me to continue my story a little further, and tell what did actually happen after I had left New York. I have been glad to obey his request; I find it pleasant to look back along the retrospect of life; each incident of the past is clothed, as Hazlitt says of Wordsworth's recollections, with the haze of imagination and has the shadowy brightness of a waking dream.

The Expatriates

I went the other day to Paddington, which is to me the most romantic of all railway stations, and whose atmosphere is enriched with memories of the valleys and streams and woods which were my haunt for so many years. What places one can reach from Paddington, and what delightful people I have met on these platforms! Here, when he was old and not very strong, I have sometimes conducted Robert Bridges, to put him in his train after a day in London; and in the immense Great Western Hotel which adjoins the station, after bidding all his London friends good-bye, Max Beerbohm would sometimes linger unaccountably for weeks, and I, who knew his secret, would sometimes meet him there.

Oxford was my destination that particular morning. I passed the stretches of the river on which I had often sailed, I saw the gardens stretching to the walls of the old house at Iffley in which I used to live, and then that view from the train of the towers and domes of Oxford which for beauty is unequaled in the world. I got out at Oxford station (a perfect station, as everything is perfect, in my opinion, on the Great Western Railway). I drove across Oxford to a little room under Magdalen tower where I was lunching; I had a glimpse of Balliol, my old college; I passed the examination buildings, the bestowal place of honors, and the lodgings of the friends I had loved. My Oxford friends were all dead or changed beyond my recognition; of college honors or university distinctions I had not the slightest thought or prospect. I felt the truth of the saying that there is no enchantment like that of disenchantment, for how enchanting was the beauty of Oxford and the journey thither, when I gazed on it all with the freedom, the indifference, the universal derision, of those who have outlived their personal desires.

I shall not preach the ephemeral nothingness which Bossuet found beneath all hope and joy: the world may be an empty bubble, as the moralists tell us; but to me, as fear and hope, desire and belief, depart, the iridescence of that bubble grows lovelier every year.

[278]

The Expatriates

I don't know how it is with other people, but in the background of my mind little scenes from the past often shine for no reason, and then for no reason they fade away. Most of the pictures on this moving panorama are insignificant enough — a heap of old stones, a gate, the forgotten turning of a road. Others are memories of more interest, and among these there shines a remembered moment when, standing on the deck of that swaying steamer in which I left New York in 1888 (all the rest of that voyage I have forgotten), I was pleasantly excited by the thought of the fate that was awaiting me beneath the ocean's eastern rim. Then I remember what did really happen, the places I went to, the friends I made during the long years of that golden age before the War: years which I spent — or, if you like, misspent — in the practice of the lovely art of writing.

Americans who go to live abroad are sometimes troubled by the word "expatriation"; they give much anxious thought to the question as to whether it is expedient, and above all whether it is right, for them to change their skies. An Englishman or other European who settles in America incurs no kind of moral blame, either in the land he has deserted or in his new-adopted home; he is supposed to have had his reasons, and it is taken for granted that they are good ones. But to desert America is somehow regarded as a kind of treachery, as if America were more than a country, were a sort of cause, and its Stars and Stripes the banner of a crusading army which it is dishonorable to desert. But is this sound doctrine? Are there not times when good citizens should change their country? Philosophy was invented after all by Ionian expatriates, Christianity developed by the Jews who left Jerusalem; the duty of any inhabitant of any country is moreover surely his duty to his own spirit; in a world which seems to be growing darker every year, he must seek the light wherever it happens to be shining. His talent, if he has a talent, must be planted in the soil and under the skies most favorable to it. Perhaps it is only such exiles and refugees, in an age where nationalism grows yearly more savage, who will keep the life of the spirit still alive.

But all that I write of expatriation is possibly out of date. It is after all fifty years since I left America, and during that period things have no doubt greatly changed. All I can say is that among my own contemporaries, those Americans who have made their home in Europe — Whistler and Henry James, Sargent and Mary Cassatt and Mrs. Wharton — are, in my opinion, more likely to be remembered than those who stayed at home.

I was told this year by an Italian friend who is now a lecturer at Harvard that there is in America a new generation of scholars and men of letters, vigorous, independent, self-reliant, original and daring in their outlook, who far surpass our older race of European scholars, and who will soon become the leaders of Western civilization. America, he says, is rapidly becoming what Germany was one hundred and fifty years ago, the centre of scholarship and thought. I should like to believe this, but there is a saying in the Bible, "By their fruits ye shall know them," which tends to make me hesitate.

If America has flowered, as it once flowered, into a mellow civilization, surely from its laden boughs should have fallen at least a few good books — books like Emerson's *Essays* or *The Scarlet Letter* or the *Leaves of Grass*, which would remain as permanent contributions to the literature of the world — books, I mean, of enduring fame and value, which, though born of an age, are destined to survive it. And with these would have appeared whole constellations of books of permanent, if not quite the same, value. Now since the death of William James (who may be regarded as the last blossom on the old New England tree), what books of this enduring quality has America produced?

When after thirty-three years abroad I did return to the United States for an operation under the hands of one of the most expert surgeons in the world, for a complaint of which I was then the victim, though most of my time was spent in the immense red building of the Johns Hopkins Hospital devoted to one of the least glorious of our human organs, I saw enough of my native country to note the disappearance of the old provincial America of my boyhood, and its replacement by the efficient civilization of the United States. This civilization did not seem to me likely to bear any of the fruits of culture which I could taste with pleasure, and I wrote a letter on the subject to the wisest man I know, who, though not an American by birth, had spent many years in the country. He wisely answered: —

ROME, *Dec.* 2, 1921

In Florence they told me that you were in America having an operation, and I am glad to hear, in spite of the delicate or indelicate character of it, you are on the way to a complete recovery. I hardly expect to be in Florence again this winter, having settled down in the sort of vulgar town hotel which I like — the Marini — to solitude in a crowd, and steady work.

This taste of mine for living in the midst of a noisy, vulgar rush of people, most of them ugly, with whom I have nothing to do, will perhaps hint to you why I am not altogether in sympathy with your judgement on America. Not that I disagree with your characterization of it ; they say it has changed even in these last ten years, but not essentially. I could perfectly recognize, though the genteel tradition may then have been stronger, that America had "no interest for the life of the mind," was "without a head," and "alien." But why do you call this condition "lying fallow" and "deterioration" ? Isn't the judgement of the American people rather the opposite, namely that its condition is constantly improving, and its labours splendidly fruitful ? Not for the "mind," which in our lips means, I suppose, the liberal or aristocratic life, the mind turned to pure reflection and pure expression and pure pleasure. But why need all the tribes of men sacrifice at our altar ? I agree that it is barbarous and tragic to strain after merely conventional ends, by attaining which nobody is the happier, but everyone is sacrificed to some fetish. But is n't America happy? The old genteel America was not happy; it was eager to know the truth, and to be "cultured," and to love "art," and to miss nothing that made other nations interesting or distinguished; and it was terribly and constitutionally unhappy, because with its handicap and its meagreness of soul and its thinness of temper and its paucity of talent, it *could* not attain, nor even approach, any of those ideals. But is the new America unhappy? Does it feel that it is living in a desert, and thirsting for the gardens and the treasure-houses of the Arabian Nights? I think not: it wants simply the sort of life it has, only more of it. It wants comfort and speed and good cheer; it wants health and spirits, and a round of weddings, football games, campaigns, outings, and cheerful funerals; and it is getting them. In the midst of this, as a sort of joke (and you may make a business of joking) there is a patter of sophomoric art and lady-like religion — never mind what, if only it is new and funny. Why not? When I was at Harvard, from my freshman days

on, I "belonged" to the *Lampoon*: and that seems
to me a sort of symbol or oracle : I belonged to the
Lampoon just as much in the philosophical faculty
as I did in the *Lampoon* "sanctum." It was all a
pleasant hard-working exuberance *by the way;*
there was not, and could not be, anything serious
or substantial in it. But notice : *all* learning and
all "mind" in America is not of this ineffectual
sophomoric sort. There is your surgeon at Baltimore who is a great expert, and *really knows how
to do things :* and you will find that, in the service
of material life, all the arts and sciences are prosperous in America. But it must be in the service
of material life; because it is material life (of
course with the hygiene, morality, and international good order that can minister to material
life) that America has and wants to have and may
perhaps bring to perfection. Think of that! If
material life could be made perfect, as (in a very
small way) it was perhaps for a moment among
the Greeks, would not that of itself be a most
admirable achievement, like the creation of a new
and superior mammal, who would instinctively
suck only the bottle ? Imagine a race perfectly

adapted to elevated railroads and aeroplanes and submarines, with a regular percentage of a neutral sex to serve as "schoolmarms," and not the least dissatisfaction with the extremes of the weather, the pains of childbirth or toothache (all pains being eliminated), or English as she is spoke by three hundred million Americans! I submit that such a race would be as well worth having and as precious in its own eyes (and any other criterion is irrelevant) as ever were the Chinese or the Egyptians or the Jews. And possibly on that basis of perfected material life, a new art and philosophy would grow unawares, not similar to what we call by those names, but having the same relation to the life beneath which art and philosophy amongst us ought to have had, but never have had actually. You see, I am content to let the past bury its dead. It does not seem to me that we can impose on America the task of imitating Europe. The more different it can come to be, the better: and we must let it take its own course, going a long way round, perhaps, before it can shake off the last trammels of alien tradition, and learn to express itself simply, not apologetically,

[287]

after its own heart. Of course, I don't mean that I feel confident that America will ever produce a true civilisation of a new sort; it may all come to nothing, as almost all experiments in nature do; but while the experiment is going on it seems only fair to give it a chance, and to watch it sympathetically.

To tell the truth, however, it is my imagination, much more than my social conscience, which is interested in the Americans who make Europe their home. Just as conquistadors set out, centuries ago, to conquer America, America now sends out conquistadors to conquer Europe: they are the true adventurers of our modern age. They have made their way and won their place in almost every country in Europe, and of every special group of artists and musicians some American is a welcome member. And among men of letters, too, they have their place. Was not Henry James a kind of king in the world of letters, and is it not to the American T. S. Eliot that our younger poets pay the sincerest praise of discipleship and admiration?

And the American women! In what capital of Europe are they not to be found reigning, if not as queens, at least as princesses? They wear ducal coronets in England, they preside at English and other embassies abroad, they are the hostesses in many Italian palaces. Seeing thus some American girl, some local Mamie or Maud or Mildred, upon her social throne in Europe, and picturing to oneself her original starting place, some main-street house perhaps where she used to sit with her beaux upon the wooden piazza or pay visits with them to the ice-cream-soda fountain round the corner, one cannot but wonder at the journey she has traveled, the transformation she has undergone, and the marvelous tact she has displayed in adjusting herself to the circumstances, the ways and manners, of that once far-away kingdom of romance which her quick intelligence has enabled her to conquer. But is not all this written in the book of Henry James?

There is of course nothing that I should like better than to write something which posterity will read. But my hope of doing so is not at all based on the various books I have already written, but rather on the books I shall write in the next twenty or thirty years. I still see myself, young and full of promise, on the threshold of a great career — I feel that the books of reference which make out that I am over seventy have made a serious mistake. But if the younger generations treat me as an old fogey I shall enjoy the privilege of the years thus bestowed upon me by denouncing them all. I am not one of those elderly sycophants and time-servers who pretend to like the young. I dislike them in many ways and disapprove of them in more. Wide and various are the themes on which I might expatiate, but as the art of letters has always been my hobby, I shall confine my diatribe to the way they write. My view is that they can't write at all. When they have scribbled down a page of newspaper English, they take no further trouble.

The Expatriates

Modern writing is mushroom writing; modern books are written for the day, and perish with it; and even while the day lasts how readily they drop from one's hands! The thought of purchasing such a book and keeping it to look at again occurs to no one, and who would dream of reading the best-seller of last year?

The truth is that almost all that makes the reading of old books delightful is neglected by those who wield their steel nibs in this age of steel. There were arts, there were blandishments, there were even tricks, which were intended to beguile the older generations, and which have succeeded in beguiling subsequent generations as well. In the first place good prose used to be written, not, as it is written to-day, for the eye alone, but also for the ear. "Write so wisely as we may," Landor makes Horne Tooke remark, "we cannot fix the minds of men upon our writings unless we take them gently by the ear." There must be suspensions, parentheses, pauses now and then for taking breath. If the

writer puts down one word after another
without regard to any consideration but that
of saying somehow what he wants to say, the
effect will be very much like that of the sentence itself — we cannot read for long such
piece-of-string sentences without boredom
and fatigue.

But not only must the respiration be considered; the ear is pleased in good writing by
variety and grace of cadence, and above all
by that personal rhythm, that song which in
a great writer is the sound of his voice and the
essence of his style. But the lack of any
rhythm in their writing is not the only fault
I find with the prose of our modern authors.
Their diction is quite as undistinguished;
they all seem to take their vocabulary from a
common dust bin. Our older writers were
lovers of language; they were fine gentlemen,
even dandies sometimes in their use of words;
they read old books and studied dictionaries
in their search for apt expressions, and now
and then on their pages we would be pleased
to see some ancient, primitive word appear

with its face washed and its eyes again shining. Or again there might be some lovely,
new-minted term to express a meaning which
had not yet found expression. One might
also come on one of those unexpected en-
counters of familiar words in which Emerson
said the art of writing consisted, or be enchanted by those longer phrases which possess a kind of magic — phrases either written
with care and deliberation as by Sir Thomas
Browne, or Pater, or sparkling sometimes
unexpectedly like those waves which break
into little gleams of foam on the ripple of
Thackeray's easy prose. But can one imagine
any one of the younger literary lions polish-
ing a phrase to make it perfect, or searching
dictionaries for the word he wants? They are
much too busy setting the world to rights
and earning comfortable incomes as they
do so.

The need for money, and plenty of it, is,
I think, one of the main reasons that the
younger generation write so badly. They no

longer find the charm, pure as a mountain spring, as Proust describes it, of being poor. I don't, however, pretend to despise money; indeed without the unfailing fountain of my little annuity how could I have ever lived? And now that I am better off, I have found it pleasant to travel in the most expensive way. Curiously enough I learnt this lesson from my cousin, Miss Thomas, who first preached to me the scorn of wealth but who, inheriting herself a large fortune at the age of sixty, spent a portion of it in expensive journeys.

She loved money, as few people I have known loved it, but the doctrine she preached to me in my youth, that it is a waste of one's life to spend it in procuring that commodity, I have never abandoned. But I no longer preach this gospel; if there is a struggle in the mind of a literary aspirant between God and Mammon, I advise that the service of the god of money should be followed — as it certainly will be followed in any case.

The pursuit of perfection is a kind of vocation, and no alternative must exist. I don't, it is true, like to see real talent prostituted, or the Muses walking the streets. When people commercialize their gifts, or make of them steppingstones to honor and success, I wish them all prosperity, but I do not find my life a blank when I am deprived of their society. If lovers of perfection cannot be found, I prefer those (but they too are a rapidly decreasing number) who have the power of sitting down morning after morning to a piece of scholarly work, done for the love of it and with no thought of immediate remuneration. But this power of self-imposed toil, and of working out of harness, seems to be denied to the younger generation. I have known a few who have tried it, but after a period of wretched idleness and self-contempt they have all returned to office stools. Birds which have tried to live on the bough in freedom, they have found their happiness at last in going back to the cage.

Having thus survived a generation which cared for the things I care for, I find that I now prefer the company of idlers and ne'er-do-wells and scalawags. I like the people who look on at life rather than those who take an active part in its business and affairs. They have plenty of leisure, and no axes to grind, which is pleasant. They don't preach at me, which is still more pleasant; and if they read at all, they read mostly old-fashioned books of the kind I like.

A Protestant controversialist of the seventeenth century once reproved the Catholics for their love of venial sins; they liked, he said, to warm themselves at fantastic fires and to dance in the light of glowworms.

This taste I share with the unreformed, at least in the idle sin of reading. I too like to dance in the light of glowworms, and the earnest and hastily written books of our modern authors are of no interest to me. So I suppose I am an old fogey, after all.

[END]

Unforgotten Years

WAS SET IN CASLON BY THE NORWOOD PRESS; PRINTED
AND BOUND BY H. WOLFF, NEW YORK, ON PAPER
MADE BY THE P. H. GLATFELTER COMPANY; BOUND
IN LINEN, AND DESIGNED BY ARTHUR WILLIAMS
SEPTEMBER MCMXXXVIII